# ACADEMY OF
# LEARNING

Your Complete Preschool Lesson Plan Resource: Volume 4

## © 2015 Breely, Crush & Associates, LLC

*Ver. 112214*

# Table of Contents

2

**Fire Safety & Fire Fighters** (continued)

# Educator Biography

Sharlit Elliott has a B.S. in Elementary Education and Early Childhood from Brigham Young University and has been a teacher for over 15 years working with children ages 3-5. She keeps current on changes in education by attending University classes and conferences several times a year. Besides having raised five children, she has held various leadership positions with the Girl Scouts and the 4-H program. She enjoys gardening, scrapbooking, reading and of course working with children.

# How to Use This Book

This book is designed for a teacher working with children ages 3-5 in a classroom, homeschool or home preschool environment. One of the most important aspects of this series is that it includes fun activities that will enhance their skills. These lessons plans, games and ideas are all for you to use. Don't forget, these are complete lessons and activities that have been designed for compliance with federal and state guidelines for education. We go above and beyond to bring you MORE than what's expected in the public school system.

We will refer to your students as "your children or class". That includes whatever area you are using these lessons for: homeschool or preschool. Our lesson plans include improving student's abilities through activities. The skills we will be working with include: listening skills, music, movement, language and literacy, mathematics, science, fine motor, creative art, sensory, dramatic play, and social skills.

The book is organized by themes which will help you quickly find just the right information. The headings in the book will direct you quickly to large group, small group, and free time activities. It will also provide ideas for field trips.

This book will include the following areas:

**Group Activities/Circle Time**

- Music & Movement is used to help develop large muscles in arms and legs. These need to be developed before children can be successful in small muscles activities such as used in writing or cutting with scissors. This area also helps children learn to enjoy music and the basics such as beat, loud/soft and fast/slow.

- Language & Literacy is how we help children learn vocabulary, story order, thinking skills, recall, concepts of the theme, and expressive language.

### Small Group Activities/Table Times

- Math & Cognitive is used to teach numbers, shapes, patterns, sorting, thinking and reasoning skills.

- Fine Motor Skills develop small muscles to be able to draw, write, manipulate small things, to tear, and to cut with scissors.

- Language & Literacy is used to develop skills such as expressive writing, visual memory, matching letters, letter sounds, categorizing items, directional words, and opposites.

- Other creative activities to develop their own uniqueness as an individual.

### Free Time

- Creative arts to draw, build, and develop their imagination.

- Sensory activities are used to learn through exploration and using their senses.

- Dramatic Play & Social Development let children take on different roles, solve problems, find solutions, and develop social interactions.

- Science helps children explore by experimenting, identifying problems, guessing what will happen, checking to see what did happen, questioning how things happened, and developing a plan of what to do next.

- Gross Motor Skills to practice using large and small muscles in fun activities.

- Field Trip Ideas to help children use real places to learn about the world.

Throughout the book we will use the following icons to show the different types of activities:

**MUSIC & MOVEMENT**

**LANGUAGE & LITERACY**

**MATH & COGNITIVE**

**FINE MOTOR SKILLS**

**CREATIVE ARTS**

**SENSORY**

**DRAMATIC PLAY & SOCIAL DEVELOPMENT**

**SCIENCE**

**GROSS MOTOR SKILLS**

**FIELD TRIP IDEAS**

## Introduction to the Units

These lesson plans have been used during the fall with great success. Because of different opinions, policies or religions, sometimes Halloween is not observed in a preschool setting. For example, in the federal Head Start programs, holidays are not observed nor are birthdays. With a mixed group of children, all the lesson plans (except Halloween) can be adjusted, modified or used to replace this particular holiday. In this way, children who do observe the holiday at home are still able to enjoy the "season" and other aspects of the holiday in a fun and safe way. Because all these topics take place in the same season, there is a little overlap from unit to unit, allowing you to pick and choose your favorite activities.

## Family Culture

## GROUP ACTIVITIES/CIRCLE TIME

### MUSIC AND MOVEMENT

"Greetings, World!" Tape from Macmillan Sing & Learn Program by Newbridge Communications, Inc. This fun song helps children how to say hello in five different languages.

"Join Hands" Tape from Macmillan Sing & Learn Program by Newbridge Communications, Inc. In this song, children learn that the earth is round and that we can do many things together. Children enjoy holding hands and going around in the circle while acting out the song.

"All Around the World" from Macmillan Sing & Learn Program by Newbridge Communications, Inc. Children act this song out and learn that all people sing, laugh and dance.

"A Wonderful Place" from Macmillan Sing & Learn Program by Newbridge Communications, Inc.

"My Family is Just Right for me" from "Barney's Favorites" Vol. 1 tape, Manufactured by Columbia House.

"Kookaburra" from "Barney's Favorites" Vol. 1 tape, Manufactured by Columbia House.

"The More We Get Together" from "Singable Songs for the Very Young" tape/CD by Raffi.

"My Dreidel" from "Singable Songs for the Very Young" tape/CD by Raffi.

"To Everyone in All the World" from "Baby Beluga" CD /tape by Raffi.

"Day O" from "Baby Beluga" CD/tape by Raffi.

"Thanks a Lot" from "Baby Beluga" CD/tape by Raffi.

"All I Really Need" from "Baby Beluga" CD/tape by Raffi.

"Kumbaya" from "Baby Beluga" CD/tape by Raffi.

"Les Petites Marionettes" from "More Singable Songs" CD/tape by Raffi.

"Sambalele" from "More Singable Songs" CD/tape by Raffi.

"You'll Sing a Song and I'll Sing a Song" from "The Corner Grocery Store" CD/tape by Raffi

"Pick a Bale O' Cotton" from "The Corner Grocery Store" CD/tape by Raffi

"Frere Jacques" from "The Corner Grocery Store" CD/tape by Raffi

"There Came A Girl From France" from "The Corner Grocery Store" CD/tape by Raffi

"We All Live Together" from "We All Live Together" Vol. 1 CD/tape by Greg Scelsa This is a great song for children to learn that we are part of the U.S.A.

"The World Is A Rainbow" from "We All Live Together" Vol. 2 CD/tape by Greg Scelsa. This is a fun song to teach that people come in different colors and when we live in harmony, the world is a beautiful rainbow of people. Children enjoy using motions while singing this song. When you come to the words "I can sing a rainbow," children put their hands up and move them back and forth to create a rainbow in the air. Then when you say the different color names, hold your fingers out and point to different fingers while saying the different colors. Next you say "world" make a circle with your arms. Now when you say "the world is a mixing cup" have one arm make a circle and the other hand pretend to stir it up. Continue making rainbows with arms and acting out the song.

"Hooray For the World" from "Teaching Peace" CD by Red Grammar. This is a fun song to march around the circle to because it has a good steady beat.

"See Me Beautiful" from "Teaching Peace" CD by Red Grammar. This song is touching and reminds everyone to look for the best in each other.

"Omi Ho'Ina" by Kani'alu Productions. This is the name of the tape album. This tape is very soothing and it would be a good choice for children to hear during free time.

During this theme be sure and invite parents into the class to teach the children special songs that represent their culture. This can be a special time for all to learn more about each other and make good memories using music to teach love.

## LANGUAGE AND LITERACY

You Are My Sunshine adapted by Steve Metzger, Scholastic INC. 2001

Grandfather and I by Helen E. Buckley, Jan Ormerod, Scholastic INC. 1994

I Love You Sticky Face by Lisa McCourt, BridgeWater Paperback 1997

All the Places to Love by Patricia MacLachlan, Scholastic INC. 1994

It Takes Two adapted by Nancy E. Krulik, Scholastic INC. 1995

The Very Little Boy by Phyllis Krasilovsky, Scholastic INC. 1992

Mommies by Dian Curtis Regan, Scholastic INC. 1996

I Love You the Purplest by Barbara M. Joosse, Scholastic INC. 1998

What Grandmas Do Best, & What Grandpas Do Best by Laura Numeroff, Scholastic INC. 2002. This is two books in one. You turn the book upside down to read the second book.

What Mommies Do Best, & What Daddies Do Best by Laura Numeroff, Scholastic INC. 2000. This is two books in one. You turn the book upside down to read the second book.

Love Is A Family by Roma Downey, Scholastic INC. 2001

I Love My Family by Wade Hudson, Scholastic INC. 1993

The Baby Sister by Tomie dePaola, Scholastic INC. 1997

Lights Out! by Angela Shelf Medearis, Scholastic INC. 2004

Whoever You Are by Mem Fox, Scholastic INC. 1997

We Are All Alike… We Are All Different by Cheltenham Elementary Kindergartners, Scholastic INC. 1991

The Legend Of The Bluebonnet by Tomie dePaola, Scholastic INC. 1989

Joseph Had a Little Overcoat by Simms Taback, Scholastic INC. 2000

Young Harriet Tubman Freedom Fighter by Anne Benjamin, Troll Associates 1992

Amazing Grace by Mary Hoffman, Scholastic INC. 1993

How Honu the Turtle Got His Shell by Turcotte McGuire, Heinemann Library, 1991

The Polynesians Knew by Tillie S Pine, McGraw-Hill, 1974

Cultures of the World – Mexico by Mary-Jo Reilly

Dropping In On Mexico by Edward K. Parker, D. King, Rourke Publishing, LLC, 2002

Teachers, if you read and discuss these books and others, children will see that it does not matter about their color of skin. They will learn that all people have love in their family and many different feelings. We do have different traditions that make us unique. It's interesting and fun to learn about each other's traditions.

This theme is more meaningful to children, if parents in your class will participate in sharing their traditions. Things to share include learning about different types of music, types of foods, clothing and how they celebrate special days. They could bring books to read to children music to sing and dance too. They also could help children make simple foods to eat, as well as make simple crafts for them to take home.

## SMALL GROUP ACTIVITIES/TABLE TIMES

### MATH & COGNITIVE

**Family Heights**

Use pictures of different family members standing or use the paper doll example and make copies of it in four sizes. Next make a set for each child in your class. Put the sheets on top of each other. Now cut through a stack of them by going around each family member in an oval or rectangle shape. Then give each child their set and have them order the sizes from smallest to largest. They will glue them onto a piece of construction paper. Children can draw faces and clothing if they would like.

**Indian Fry Bread**

Teacher assembles these ingredients:        Add:

6 cups flour                                 Water until mixture forms stiff dough.

1 ½ Tablespoons salt                         Knead until dough is thick and elastic.

1 ½ Tablespoons baking powder                Form into thin round patties. Fry in ½
                                             inch oil until brown on each side.

Children will wash their hands for this activity. Make a large copy of the recipe for the children to follow along with the numbers of each item. Children will take turns adding the ingredients and all children will count the numbers of the cups of flour together. They will each take a turn stirring the mixture. Each child will be given a small amount of the dough to knead. Teacher will fry the fry bread with the children kept back enough so they won't get burned. When they are cooked, place them on paper towels to cool. Next children can eat with butter or put canned chili with tomatoes, lettuce and cheese on top.

**Japanese Fan Counting**

Draw a small fan such as the example below and copy it ten times on colored paper. Now put the numerals 1-10 on each fan front and dots or small sticker flowers on the back of the fans. Use the same amount of dots/stickers as the numeral written on the front of the fan.

Mix up the fans so that they are not in order. Children will take turns picking a fan and telling what number is on the front of the fan. If they do not recognize the number have them turn the fan over and count the dots/stickers to correctly identify the numeral. Keep taking turns counting and naming numerals until all of the fans have been used.

Now have the children take turns using the back of the fans to order them starting with number one. Number them using the sticker or dot side up. Next to it place the fan with two stickers/dots. Children continue ordering them until they reach all ten objects in their correct order.

Then on another day have them try to order the fan using the front numerals. If they still need some help let them turn over the fan to count the dots/stickers to place them in correct order.

## Gingerbread Families

Use the following recipe with children. Have them count and measure each ingredient as they follow the large copy of the recipe. (Make sure that they wash first.)

| | |
|---|---|
| 2 cups flour | 1 Tbsp. ground cinnamon |
| 1 cup salt | 2 Tbsp. ground ginger |
| 2 Tbsp. ground allspice | 2 Tbsp. vegetable oil |
| 1 cup water | |

Put all the ingredients in a large bowl. Then have the children mix them. Next, divide up the dough among the children, so that they can all help knead the dough until it is smooth. Now have the children roll the dough into thin slices and provide small and large sized gingerbread cookie cutters. Have children cut out their family. An optional decoration to do would be to provide small wiggle plastic eyes and small buttons or beads. Use a large foam plate with their names on it to place their completed family to take home. These families are for fun decoration and not to eat.

## Mexican Dessert

Teacher will buy a package or two of soft tortillas or children will make their own tortillas.

Tortillas
| | |
|---|---|
| 4 cups flour | 1/4 cup shortening |
| 2 tsp. salt | 1 Tb. baking powder |
| warm water | |

Combine all ingredients except water. Then use your clean hands to break up shortening into the flour for about one minute. Then slowly add warm water. Stir dough and when it's stiff take it out of the bowl. Place it on a floured board or table and knead it until dough is smooth. Break it off into small size roll size. Shape it into a ball and roll it out to form a circle. Then cook it on a grill over medium heat. Turn it one or two times.

Dessert

Have on hand vegetable oil, cinnamon and some sugar. Heat electric fry pan with ½ inch of oil in it. Keep children back from the hot oil and pan.

Children will use a plastic knife to cut their circle shell into wedges. Children will choose to cut it into 4, 5 or 6 pieces. They will count them. Then they will give their slices to the teacher to cook in the hot oil.

Have each child again count their pieces to you before cooking them. When the shell has been in the hot oil for a minute or so and is puffed up, teacher will take pieces out and place on a paper plate. After it cools slightly, child will sprinkle sugar and cinnamon on it and eat it.

## Hawaiian "Wish" Cake

Children will help make this cake by adding the ingredients while counting and measuring them. They will help mix, crack the eggs and open the packages. Optionally, you could make these into cupcakes so that the children can add the paper cups into the muffin pan and put their own batter into the paper liner cup. When it has been cooked they can put the icing on their own to eat and enjoy. Be sure and make a large copy of the recipe for the children to follow. The numeral recognition is important as well as seeing the words that you follow. This helps them know that reading is important!

1 pkg. (3 1/4 oz.) coconut pudding
1cup water
1 pkg. (1 lb., 2.5 oz.) white cake mix
½ cup salad oil
4 eggs
1 can white frosting mix
1 cup shredded coconut

Preheat oven to 350 degrees. Grease and flour a 13x9x2 cake pan or use cupcake paper liners. In a small bowl, soften pudding in water. In a mixing bowl, beat cake mix and oil; add eggs and beat 4 minutes. Add softened pudding; mix well. Pour into prepared pan or cupcake liners. Bake for cake for 35-40minutes or cupcakes for 25-30 minutes. Cool on cake rack. Put frosting mix onto cake or cupcakes and sprinkle with shredded coconut.

## ✂ FINE MOTOR SKILLS

### Sombrero Collage

Teacher makes sombrero pattern such as the example for each child in the class. Put pattern on top of five plan sheets and cut along lines. Then add the lines for the parts of the sombrero. An optional way would be to make sombrero pattern and make copies on a copy machine of it. Then have the children cut out their own sombrero on the lines. Now have available feathers, beads or small foam shapes to glue onto the sombrero.

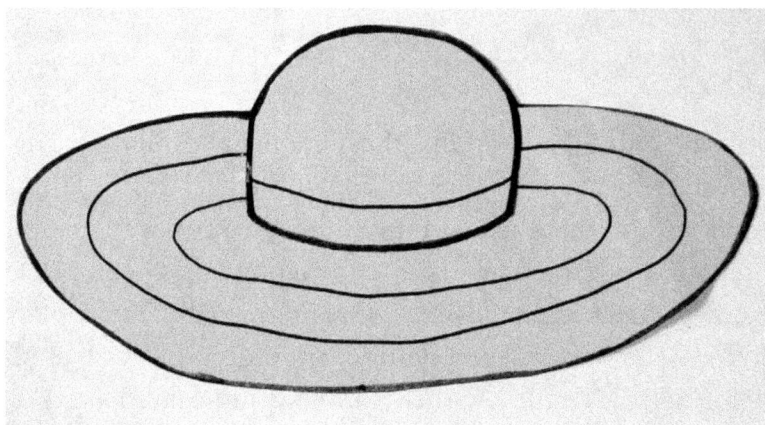

### Child Sombrero

Go to a paper supply or school supply store and buy colored butcher paper for this project. You will need to cut paper into about 1 yard lengths for each child to have a hat. You will also need a roll of masking tape, glue, feathers, and various craft items for decorations.

Begin this activity with the child sitting on a chair. The teacher or other helper places the cut length of paper over the child's head with child's head in the middle of the paper. Then the teacher firmly gathers the middle paper around the top of the child's head closely to conform around it. If you have a helper, then she/he uses the masking tape to wrap around and around to form the crown of the hat. If you have no helper, do the best you can to tape it and hold the gathers to form the crown.

Next firmly take the loose ends of paper and roll it up to form a brim around the whole outside of the hat. Lastly, the child goes to the table and writes his/her name on the sombrero and glues decorations around the hat. When the glue is dry, they can wear it and take it home.

## Indian Sand Painting

You can prepare children for this activity by checking out books to show Indian paintings or use actual objects with Indian paintings on them. Then prepare the colored sand. You can buy colored sand or make your own by mixing powdered tempera paint with while sand or salt. Put each color of sand in a shaker bottle such as a pepper shaker or an empty spice shaker.

Pass out sheets of construction paper and small bottles of glue. Children will make their own Indian painting by using the glue to create designs like the ones shown earlier. Then place the drawings on trays and sprinkle the colored sand over the wet glue. Shake off the excess glue of one color before adding the next color of sand. Now leave them to dry and let the children take them home when dry. See example.

## Indian Sand Jars

Ask parents to save small baby food jars for this activity for you. Obtain colored sand or make your own as in "Indian sand painting". Obtain funnels to use for filling the jars. The Dollar Store has packages of 4 in a set of different sizes. Also, buy candle wax at a craft store. Set out trays for children to fill their bottles on. Use a can inside a pan with water it to melt the wax on a low temperature on the stove or a hot plate. Watch the level of the water carefully to prevent fire and/or accidents.

Children will pick three colors to place in their jars. They will place their jars on a tray and put the funnel inside them. Then they will carefully spoon one color of sand into the jar until it is about 1 ¼ inches deep. Then they will pour the extra sand that may have spilled back into the bowl of colored sand before adding the next color of sand.

They will continue by filling the jar with a different color of sand until they have reached the 1 ¼ inch mark. They will use the same procedure each time they change colors as before when they disposed of the extra sand. If the bottle is larger it may need either deeper sand or more colors to fill it. Please adjust it according to size of the jar.

When all the sand has been layered into the bottle and it has reached the top, pour the melted wax to seal it. The layers will stay separated with a reasonable amount of care.

## Mexican Flag

Children will use a piece of white construction paper for the flag. They will cut a green piece of paper and a red piece of paper 4 inches wide by about 9 inches long. These rectangle pieces will be glued on to the white page, one at each end of the sheet. The emblem shown in the example should be glued on the white section in the middle of the flag. The left side of the flag is green and the right side is red.

The following is the story of how the flag came about.

A long time ago, the Aztecs lived in the northern part of Mexico. An Aztec legend told that as the Aztecs moved southward they would come to a place that had a lake and some good farm land. It would be there that they would see an eagle perched on a cactus with a snake in its mouth. They were to settle there. One day, a group of Aztecs came upon the exact place that had been described to them. They decided to settle there and to make their home. Today, the home of the Aztecs is said to be the site of Mexico City and the eagle on the flag represents strength and nobility, the snake represents evil and dishonor and the cactus is for the Mexican soil. The evergreen oak and laurel branch represent the heroes of Mexico.

## Japanese Lantern

Prepare enough red and yellow paper for each child to have one piece of each color. Teacher will also supply a 1 ½ inch stripe of black paper which is 9 inches long for each child's handle. Fold the red pieces of paper in half lengthwise. Draw lines from the fold down to within one inch from the bottom of the open ended page. Continue to draw lines across the page until the other end of the paper has been reached. Use a paper cutter to cut across the yellow paper making it 2 inches shorter than the red paper.

Children will leave the paper folded over and cut on the lines until they reach the end of the each line being careful to only go to the end of the line. Now children will unfold their lantern and over lap the two red sheet ends to form a cylinder. Teacher will help them staple the ends together. Next the yellow paper will be rolled to form a cylinder shape and placed inside the red lantern and stapled to the top and bottom of the red sheet. This will leave a permanent fold in the red paper to give the appearance of the lantern being lit. Then the black handle will be stapled to the top of both sides of the lantern. Hang these lanterns from the ceiling using clear fish line attached to a thumb tack. See example.

## Japanese Fans

Give each child a piece of paper and tell them to create a picture or design on each side of the paper using crayons or markers. When they have finished drawing, help them fold their papers using a 1 ½ wide fold. Fold the paper back and forth forming an accordion type of fold. Next, the teacher will fold the fan lengthwise one time and staple it by the one center fold to a wide tongue depressor stick. Then open up the fan on both sides and pull the fan side down to meet at the bottom and staple them to the stick. Hold the fan by the end wood piece and cool off with a great fan. See example.

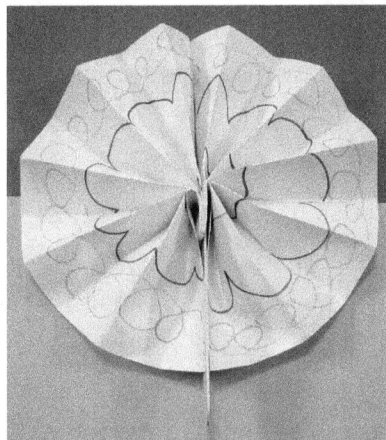

## Chopstick Fun

Buy some inexpensive wood chopsticks at an Asian store or from a restaurant. Show the children how to use them and then provide an easy food such as cheerios in a small bowl for them to practice eating. Children put their used chopsticks in back pack to take home after eating, so they don't share germs.

## Honu The Turtle

Read the book of <u>How Honu the Turtle Got His Shell</u> by Turcotte McGuire and then do this fun project with the children.

Draw the turtle shape like example below and put pattern on top of five sheets of green construction paper. Staple the edges and cut out the turtle shape. Continue in this manner until there you have one for each child. Use the paper cutter to cut a one inch strip of different bright colors of paper. Set the turtle patterns, strips of colored paper, small wiggle plastic eyes and the glue out on the table.

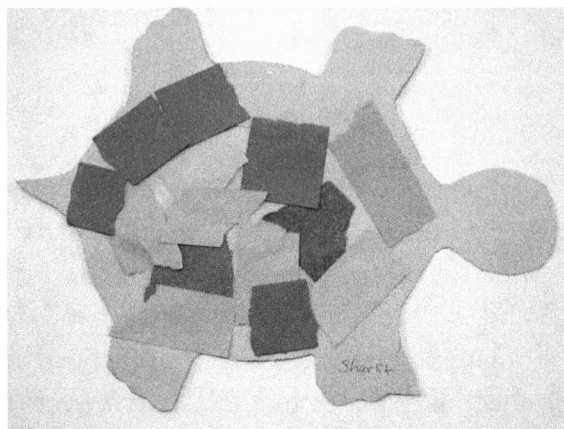

Children will tear the strips to form the decoration of the turtle shell and glue them on it, along with the wiggle eyes. Have a few markers available so that they can draw any other details that they would like.

## Uncle Sam

Have parents save empty toilet paper rolls to use for this activity. Buy large wiggle eyes, blue felt or foam, skin colored felt or foam and holiday wide ribbon with red, white, blue and if possible, with small stars on it. If you plan ahead, this type of ribbon can be found in craft stores around the 4th of July. Also buy white wavy chenille pipe cleaners. You will need only one piece of wavy chenille for each child. The chenille should be cut between each small part and then cut it in half. This forms the eyebrows. Cut the skin colored material large enough to wrap around the roll and overlap a little. Cut the ribbon the size needed to wrap around the toilet paper roll plus a little to overlap. Make a three inch circle of the blue for the hat. Next put the toilet paper roll in the center of the circle and trace the circle. Cut it out of the middle of the blue circle. This will be the top of the top hat and the circle with the cut out middle will be the band of the hat.

1. Put glue on the skin colored material wrapping it around the whole roll with a little overlap.

2. Glue on the ribbon and then put it around the end of the toilet paper roll over lapping it a little. 3- Put the blue rim on the roll and pull it down until it is at the end of the ribbon.

4. Place glue around the bottom edge of the hat rim.

5. Glue around the top edge of the toilet paper roll forming the top of the hat.

6. Glue the chenille eyebrows on under the hat rim.

7. Glue on the eyes. Now it's ready to dry and take home.

See example below.

## LANGUAGE AND LITERACY

### Show and Tell

Have different parents come in each day and bring in objects, foods and/or clothing and show the children the items. Encourage the children ask questions about what they see. Have the child from that family tell about what they like best about their family and what some of their favorite foods are.

If parents can't come in to share, ask if they will send items in to show. Also ask them to write up something to share with the children about the items sent.

## Tasting Table

Bring in fresh fruits like mangos, papaya, bananas and pineapple for the children to taste. Ask them where they think the fruits grow, how they grow and what they taste like. Then have the children taste them. Ask the children tell you how they taste - example soft, sour, sweet.

## Family Photos

Ask parents to send in copies of family photos along with a short narrative about their family. Take turns on different days having that child show his/her photos and telling about the people in their family. The teacher will also read the family's narrative to the children.

## Story Comparison

Read the story of The Three Little Javellinas by Susan Lowell. Then have the children tell you the story of The Three Little Pigs, the traditional version. Ask the children to tell you what things are a like about the two stories and then ask them to tell you what things are different in the two stories.

## Animals From Other Nations

Read the book Snap! By Marcia Vaughan. After reading the story, talk about the character or personality of Joey, Twisker, Slider, Flatso, Prickler and the Sly-tooth. After asking questions about each of them, go to the last page and show their pictures while reading what the species they are, their animal class, their favorite food and their special feature.

## Children Positions

Have children follow your directions such as line up one behind the other, beside - give a child's name, in front of give - a child's name, under a their arms (give names), hand over head (child's name) and etc. Then let the children take turns tell others where to go and what to do. They can not point or say over there. They must use position names.

## FREE TIME

### CREATIVE ARTS

Draw and cut out large shirts and dresses out of butcher paper. Children will water color flowers on them or whatever they want to represent how people dress. See examples below.

Teacher will provide markers, different colors of construction paper, scissors and glue so that children can design their own flag.

### SENSORY

Place in the table mixed grains with plastic little people, plastic pet animals and berry baskets to represent houses.

Put play dough in the sensory table with scissors to cut dough.

## DRAMATIC PLAY & SOCIAL DEVELOPMENT

Organize prop boxes with different culture clothing in each box. One box will have leis and grass skirts with flowers for their hair and flower shirts. One easy way to acquire the grass skirts and the leis would be to order them at the inexpensive prices offered from the Oriental Trading catalog. You can reach them on the Internet at www.orientaltrading.com. You may pick up other items of clothing at your local thrift store. You can even sew some up by buying patterns and material when they go on sale.

Another prop box could contain sombreros, maracas, fiesta lanterns and colorful piñata. You can also buy these items at www.orientaltrading.com. It would also be a good idea to ask parents if you could borrow any of their Mexican items that would not be easily broken. You could also look at the thrift store for long skirts that you could add ruffles to the hems or Ponchos that just need some bright colors added to them.

One other prop box could contain Native American clothing. Check the Halloween patterns at the material stores for a simple Indian dress patterns and vest patterns with fringe endings on them. String some seeds together for necklaces and buy some fake turquoise for added jewelry. Look for moccasins and other items at the thrift store.

Children will enjoy trying on the different clothing and pretending to be someone different than they are now.

## SCIENCE

Display a rock collection with labels on the rocks or by them. Also have magnifier glass so that the children can examine them closely. You can buy small rocks at local earth museums or start your own collection. Buy or check out a picture book on rocks and minerals from the library. Put books from the library on the science table with the rocks. Posters on rocks are also available at school supply stores.

## GROSS MOTOR SKILLS

Go to the library and ask the librarian to help you find a tape or CD with the <u>Mexican Hat Dance</u> on it and take it to school and teach them to do the hat dance. You could also look for the song <u>La Bamba</u> on a tape or CD and have the children dance around to it while shaking maracas.

While at the library look for the Hawaiian <u>Hukilau</u> song, so the children can have fun doing the hula to it.

Another fun thing to do would be to find the <u>Limbo</u> song and put a broom over the top of two chairs and have the children do the limbo to the music.

Another song that is fun to have the children dance to is called <u>The Chicken Dance</u> look for it while at the library too.

### Chippewa Serpentine Dance

This is a fun dance that the Indians do. The first thing you do is learn the "Toe-Heel Step." Teacher plays a 1-2 beat on a drum with her hand using a loud and then a soft beat. On the loud beat of the drum, the dancers step up with the left foot and touch the ground lightly with the toe. On the soft beat, come down hard on the heel. Do this first with the left foot and then with the right foot, moving around forward, backward and in a circle.

When the children have learned to do these steps, choose a leader to lead the dance. Everyone follows the leader and does the toe heel step and dances around in a large circle. Then the leader forms a large figure eight and the dancers weave in and out as they follow their leader.

## FIELD TRIP IDEAS

Check with your local Colleges to see if they have international days or special culture days. If so, find out when they are and find out if there will be an opportunity for the children to attend some of the activities.

Check with local High Schools and see if they have any special language activities connected with their foreign language classes. If so, find out if any would be appropriate for the children in your class and make arrangements to go if they are appropriate. If not, ask if any students would be willing to come to your school and share their language and any visuals that would be interesting to the children who are in preschool. They could teach them a few greetings too.

Another idea would be to go on a neighborhood walk and observe the different colors of the houses and the different types of materials that they have been constructed out of.

# Fire Safety & Fire Fighters

## GROUP ACTIVITIES/CIRCLE TIME

### MUSIC AND MOVEMENT

"Stop, Drop, Rock 'n' Roll" from Macmillian Sing & Learn Program by Newbridge Communications, Inc. Children have a great time acting this song out with its great up-beat music.

"911" from Macmillian Sing & Learn Program by Newbridge Communications, Inc. Children really enjoy learning when to call 911 and they enjoy pretending to dial the number.

"Fire Fighters!" from Macmillian Sing & Learn Program by Newbridge Communications, Inc. Children pretend to be fire fighters and they put out the fire and drive to the next fire in their fire trucks.

"The Freeze" from "We All Live Together" tape/CD by Greg Scelsa. This song teaches children to stand still and not move at all them the word "freeze" is said. It is a fun song that also includes a lot of fun movement in it, but the quiet freeze part could help in an emergency. The children would stay very still and listen, so you could give clear instructions to them.

**"Bingo"** A Traditional song changed a little by Sharlit Elliott.

There was a fire-man had a dog

and Bin-go was his name-o.

B-I-N-G-O, B-I-N-G-O, B-I-N-G-O,

and Bin-go was his name-o.

Sing whole song 6 times and then verses 2-6 you will leave out a letter and clap it its place.

2.  Clap-I-N-G-0 (Clap on B)

3.  Clap-Clap-N-G-O

4.  Clap-Clap-Clap-G-O

5.  Clap-Clap-Clap-Clap-O

6.  Clap-Clap-Clap-Clap-Clap

For this song, use a die-cut to punch out five hand prints or trace a hand print and cut it out. Then mount each hand print on a rectangle piece of heavy paper. On the other side of each hand print place one of the letters that is used to spell bingo. Now laminate them. When you sing the song, point to the letters on the cards. When you leave a letter out, turn the card over of that letter to show the hand print. Then when children see the hand print they will know to clap. This song is a fun way to learn to follow directions and learn letter names. You could change the name of the dog to any five letter name that you would like.

"Firefighters" from book <u>More Piggyback Songs</u> compiled by Jean Warren, Totline Press, Warren Publishing House, 1984

"I Am A Fireman" from book <u>More Piggyback Songs</u> compiled by Jean Warren, Totline Press, Warren Publishing House, 1984

They enjoy all these songs very much and want to sing them over and over again. Add words to nursery rhyme tunes and write your own songs to fit want you want them to learn. You already know the tunes so it's not hard and have fun.

## LANGUAGE AND LITERACY

Fire! Fire! by Gail Gibbons, Scholastic Inc., 1992. In this book, children will learn how fire fighters battle a blaze in the city, the country, the forest, and on the water.

Fire Fighter! by Angela Royston, DK Publishing, Inc., 1998. This book describes a day in the life of a fire fighter.

Dot the Fire Dog by Lisa Desimini, from book Scholastic Inc., 2001. This book has large pictures and show life at a fire house from a dog's prospective.

Corduroy Goes to the Fire Station by Don Freeman, Scholastic Inc. 2003. This book has great pictures and it has many lift the flap pages for children to lift to see what is behind the flap.

The Story of Smokey Bear by Robin Bromley, Ladybird Books USA, 1996. This is where Smokey tells us that only you can prevent forest fires.

A Day With Firefighters by Jan Kottke, Scholastic Inc., 2002. This book has real photos of firefighters.

At the Firehouse by Anne Rockwell, Scholastic Inc., 2003. This book has dogs being the fire fighters. It is a cute book and you can buy a tape of the story as well.

Officer Buckle and Gloria by Peggy Rathmann, Scholastic Inc., 1996. This book teaches in a funny way that safety rules help us be safe, for example, we don't play with matches.

Dinofours It's Fire Drill Day! by Steve Metzger, Scholastic Inc. 1997. In this book Mrs. Dee, the preschool teacher, helps Albert overcome his fear of the loud noise of the fire bell by explaining that fire drill keeps children safe. It includes fire safety tips. This book is a must before you have your first fire drill.

Children really enjoy these books, but don't forget to ask many open ended questions about each book. This helps children to learn to express themselves to others. It also helps to ask children to listen carefully and report back to you at the end of the book their favorite parts. Listening for a purpose helps them to develop comprehension skills.

Curious George by H.A. Rey, Scholastic Inc. 1941.

Curious George At the Fire Station, adapted from the Curious George film series, edited by Margret Rey and Alan J. Shalleck, Houghton Mifflin Company Boston, 1985.

Clifford the Firehouse Dog by Norman Bridwell, Scholastic Inc. 1994.

# SMALL GROUP ACTIVITIES/TABLE TIMES

## MATH & COGNITIVE

### Fire House Dog Game

Use a coloring book to find a dog pattern or draw your own like the example. Make five or six dog pictures on white paper. These will be the game cards so laminate them. Obtain a bag of black pompoms. The pompoms can be small or medium in size. The size of the pompom depends on the size of the dog pattern you are using. The larger the dog, the bigger the pompoms should be. Prepare 2x2 inch squares and make two sets of the numerals 1- 5 on them.

Children will each have a dog game card. Black pompoms will be used for the dots that they will place on their dog. There will be a bowl of dots in the middle of the table for all to reach.

Children will take turns drawing number squares. The number on their card indicates how many dots they should take to put on their dog. Each time they draw a card they will say the number on their card. If they need help knowing which number it is have other children help them or teacher will help them. Then they will count out that number of dots and place them on their dog.

Children will continue to play by taking turns until all on the cards have been used. Next, children with the teacher will count how many dots are on their dog. Play this game throughout the week and it will help them with counting and number recognition.

## Match the Number

Buy stickers or use a die cut of a fire hat of other type of sticker such as a fire truck or safety badge to make cards. Make the fire hat die cut on colored paper or use a picture sticker and place it on a square of heavy weight paper. Make a matching one and put matching numerals on the squares of fire hats. Use numeral set from 1-5 until children have these recognized well. Then use 1-10 for a more advanced time. Put the cards facing up on the table and have children take turns making a match with identical numbers. Play continues until all cards have been used up. See example.

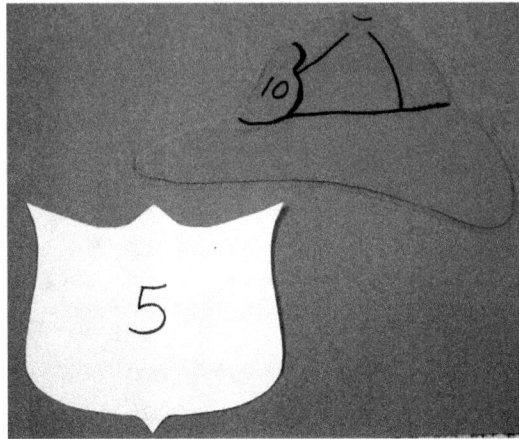

## Game 2

Use the same cards as in "match the numbers" activity, but this time have the cards placed down. Children will take turns drawing three cards and trying to remember where the matching cards are located. If no match, the player will put the cards back down where they found them. Then the next person takes their turn and tries to make a match. When a person makes a match, that person says the number that is on the matching cards and gets to take another turn. When the person does not make a match the next person takes a turn. Play continues until all the cards have been matched up. Then the players will count up their matches one child at a time with others counting with him/her.

## Order the Hoses

Cut an old hose into sizes from small to large. Make each set of hoses four or five pieces. The teacher will give each of the children a set of hoses and when she says "go" the children will try and be the first ones to get their hoses in the correct order from largest to smallest. If one of the children is having trouble doing this activity, adjust it while he/she is at your table to just do three hoses. All the children will just do three when that child is there. Then if they can do it add another hose and do it again.

## Pattern Fire Hats

Use stickers or die cut punches to make patterns. You will need one design in four different colors for children to make a four pattern line. They can also use stickers mounted on squares of four different fire fighter items like truck, boot, hose, and hat. There are many different types of stickers at scrap booking stores and school supply stores from which to choose. These stores also carry die cut machines that you can usually use for free if you purchase your paper there. When the materials have been prepared, give children a model to see a three pattern and a four pattern example. Then give each child a narrow long piece of paper in a suitable size to mount their pattern pieces. Have them make their pattern on the table before gluing it to their paper. Help them with layout on the table if needed, but then let them do it on their own when gluing it.

## Safety Rules Game

Make a game board with squares to move players from a starting position to a finished position. See example. Then make cards that ask questions such as: What would you do if you found matches? If you see a fire in your house who should you tell? If there aren't any big people at home and you see smoke or fire in your house where should you go? What is the number you call in case of an emergency? If your clothes catch on fire what should you do? If you see someone playing with matches or a lighter what should you do? If you have a fire should you stop and get your toys before leaving the house? What is a meeting plan? Can you tell one way to leave your house in an emergency?

Mount these questions and any other ones that you wish to review with the children in your class with numerals from 1-5 on each card. Then laminate the cards. Also make a few cards that say, "reward card - move ahead (1-3) a numeral of spaces to move.

Children will receive a game token to move around the board. This could be a button or if possible a small fire engine (find in party favors). Tell children they will draw a card and if they answer the card correctly they may move ahead the space number found on that card. Children will continue taking turns until they reach the finish place.

**Phone**

Prepare a phone pattern such the example for each child to trace around or that parents have prepared. Type large numbers 9, 1, 1 in a set for each child's use. Also have scissors and glue ready for children to use.

Children will place their tracer on their choice of colored paper and trace around edges and cut it out. Then they will cut their strip of numbers apart and glue them in the center of their phone. Next, they will tell the teacher the numeral names and when you should call those numbers. Also review with them when not to call those numbers.

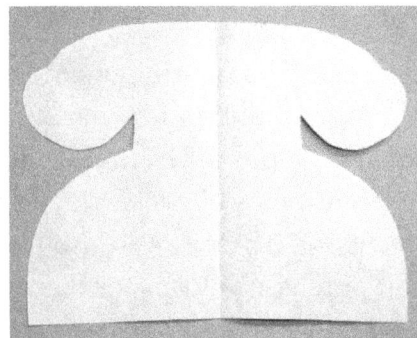

## FINE MOTOR SKILLS

**Fire Dog**

Make a dog ear pattern such as the example on a folded piece of colored construction paper. This will be the dog's ears. Either provide a pattern for children to trace the ear on a folded page, or have parents trace them. Also cut a 2 to 2 ½ inch wide long strip of paper. This will be the head band.

Then give each child the folded page and tell them to cut on the lines to make their dog ears. Tell them to keep it folded while cutting, so they will have two ears. Next have children draw dots on their ears with markers, crayons or use bingo dot markers. Now staple the ears onto the head band and make a circle with the band to fit around each child's head and staple it closed.

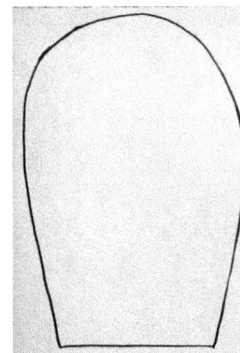

**Safety Badge**

**1st Activity:** Make patterns of a large badge. See example. Children will trace around the badge pattern and then cut it out. Have a variety of small objects for children to collage on the badge such as colored noodles, small foam shapes, beads or etc.

**2nd Activity:** Instead of the collage, have children write their name in the middle of the badge and then use glue to make lines around the edges of the badge. Next, they will place their badge on a tray and sprinkle it with glitter. When the glue is all covered with glitter, have them carefully dump the extra glitter off onto the tray and leave it on a flat surface to dry.

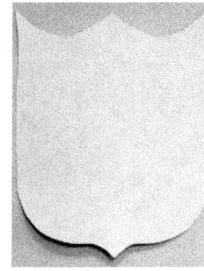

## Firefighter Puppet

Provide white lunch sacks for the children to use for this activity. Also set out markers, glue and scissors for the children. Make a fire hat pattern such as the one below for children or parent to trace on red construction paper.

Children will use the markers to draw a large face on the top folded end of their lunch sack. Then each child will receive a traced fire hat or will trace their hat. Then they will cut out their hat on the lines and glue it around the face they have drawn on their sack puppet. They can play with their puppet as soon as it is dry.

## Dot Dog

Use the large dot dog pattern idea from math activity "Fire House Dog Game". Make a dog for each child in your class. Provide markers, crayons, or bingo dot markers. Also provide short pieces of ribbon for collar, large button for tag and large wiggles plastic eyes. Children will decorate their dog as desired with the materials.

## Fire Engine

Make a basic engine pattern such as the one below. Children or parents will trace the pattern onto red construction paper. Children will cut it out. Teacher will use circle die cut or large circle paper punch make wheels from black construction paper. Make

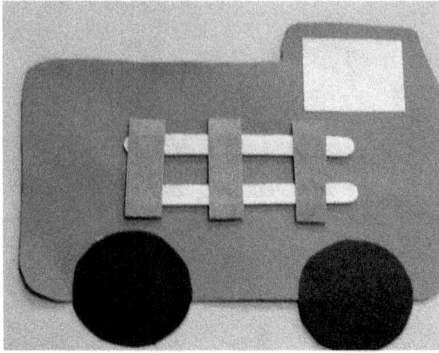

enough wheels for each child to have two wheels. Provide two craft sticks for each child to form the ladder sides, along with brown paper for them to create their own rungs for their ladder. Yellow paper will also be provided so children can cut their own window, along with brown paper for them to create their own rungs for their ladder.

## Smokey the Bear

Teacher will provide a bear head pattern for children or parents to trace on brown construction paper. See example. Children will cut their bear head out and use markers to draw a face on the bear. They could also glue large wiggle eyes on the bear.

For the back of the bear, print a copy of the song "Smokey the Bear," so children can sing the song with parents help.
Singing it in class helps them learn the tune, but they will probably need help with the words and parents can do that.

**Smokey the Bear** – by Steve Nelson and Jack Rollins

Smokey - the bear, Smokey - the Bear.

Prowlin' and growlin' and a sniffin' - the air.

He can find a fire - before it starts to flame.

That's why they call him Smokey,

that was how he got his name.

**LANGUAGE AND LITERACY**

### House Fire

Have craft sticks, pieces of orange, yellow and red paper and glue available for children's use. Children will use craft sticks on white paper to form a house and glue it to the paper. Then they will tear pieces of orange, yellow and red paper to make fire flames. They will glue these flames to part of the house. Ask children to tell you how you how the fire may have started and write their words on the page. Also ask them to tell you how they will keep safe if there is a fire and write these words also. See example below.

### Crayon Melting

Have one or two food warming trays at the table with crayons and paper. These can be found online or at a thrift store for very little money. Place a paper grocery bag on top of the warmer and then place a white piece of paper over the bag. Teacher will then demonstrate using a crayon on the paper. Tell the children not to touch the warmer because it is hot. This activity needs to be carefully supervised.

The crayon will melt onto the paper. Note the tray gets very warm, but it won't burn you unless touching it for a long period of time. But won't tell the children that or they might not be careful. Let them write their name on a paper. Then discuss how fire can hurt you and have them review all the safety rules they have talked about at circle time. Be sure and have them take turns speaking so they all can have an opportunity to talk.

## Fire Fighter, Fire Fighter

In this language activity children will be learning and reviewing color names. Make a house pattern and then copy it on different pieces of colored paper or color each house a different color. Then cut the houses out and laminate them. You will also need to draw, color, cut and laminate a fire fighter.

Hold up each house one at a time and call on a child to tell the color of the house. Continue asking colors of houses until all the colors of the houses have been named. Then the teacher will put on the table three or four of the colored houses. The teacher will tell the children that the fireman is going to go into one of the houses to look for a fire.

Children will close their eyes while the teacher puts the fire fighter under one of the houses. Then children will open their eyes. Next the children will chant these words with the teacher – "Fire fighter, fire fighter which color house has the fire?"

Children will be called on one at a time to guess which house the fire fighter is in. After the child names a colored house he/she can pick up the house to see it the fire fighter is under/ in that house. If that child does not guess correctly, then another child guesses. Play continues until the fire fighter has been found.

Now, put away those houses and set out three or four different colored houses. Children will close their eyes again while the teacher hides the fire fighter. Play continues again with different children guessing the color of the house that the fire fighter is in. Keep playing this game until all the colored houses have been used and all the children have had many turns to name the colored houses. See example.

## Position Fire Fighters

Use small plastic fire fighters from toy or dollar stores or make copies of fire fighter used in "Fire Fighter, Fire Fighter" activity. Each child will need their own fire fighter and a house.

To make the houses for the children to use in this activity use house from the "Fire Fighter, Fire Fighter" activity, increase its size and tape it to a small shoe box or other small square box. The door on the house should be cut open, so the fire fighter can go inside the house.

Tell the children to put the fire fighter inside the house, outside the house, under the house, over the house, beside the house, in front of the house, and behind the house. Teacher will ask children to say the words of where to put the fire fighter with her. Then children will take turns telling others where to put their house the same way that the teacher modeled the words. Pay continues until all the children have had a turn being the leader that tells them where to put their fire fighter.

## Equipment

Obtain pictures or where possible, actual items that fire fighters use such as the following: fire hydrant, fire extinguisher, hose, ax, ladder, and fire clothing such as hat, coat, mask, boots, gloves, and uniform. Teacher will show each item or picture of item and invite children to take turns telling what they know about each them. When they have all had a turn, invite them to ask you questions that they might have about the items. Make sure that children learn how and why each item is used and why they need the items.

Read the simple book <u>A Day With Firefighters</u> by Jan Kottke. Then ask the children to take turns telling you what they liked about the book and what their favorite parts were. Ask if they would like to visit a fire station, and if so what questions they would like to ask the fire fighters. Write down all their questions with their names and tell them that you will try and make arraignments for them to visit a fire station and that you will give the fire fighters their questions to answer.

## Sequence Cards

Make four cards that tell a story in obvious sequence such as matches laying on floor, a child picking up matches, small fire on floor, smoke and flames. You can use stick figures for drawing or use magazine pictures to tell any story that you would like. Put each picture on an index card and laminate them. Mix the cards up and have children take turns telling what is happening in each picture. Now have them figure out what happened first and then what happened and so on. If they get one wrong, have them re-state what is happening in the picture before. Then have them look at the pictures that are left and figure out the correct next picture. Have the children answer questions to help guide them.

## CREATIVE ARTS

Make a drawing of a large fire fighter's boot for a pattern and then make copies of it by placing pattern on top of ten pieces of water color paper and cutting through all thicknesses at once. Continue this process until you have enough for all the children to have at least one of them. Then place the boots on the easel for the children to watercolor or put poster paint out for them to use on the boots. See example.

Post simple pictures of fire trucks, fire hydrants and people watching fires. Put paper on the easel near pictures to inspire the little artists. Have paper with markers available for them to use along with crayons and paint.

## SENSORY

Fill empty fine mist spray bottles with water and place them in the sensory tub. Make foam flames of yellow, red and orange. Tape the flames to the bottom of the tub. Children will use the spray bottles to pretend to put out the flames. Explain to the children before time to use them, that the spray bottles are only to be sprayed at the flames or the bottles will be put away. This activity promotes the development of fine motor skills.

Another day, use sand in the sensory table with little people, toy fire engines, trucks, craft sticks for fences and small bocks and/or Lincoln logs that children can use to build houses or buildings.

## DRAMATIC PLAY & SOCIAL DEVELOPMENT

Supply a box of fire fighter props such as fire hat and slicker. You can buy them sometimes at dollar stores or other toy stores. Also, save that old hose to cut short pieces to have the children use to out the fire. Other items you can make are oxygen tanks made from large empty pop bottles. Cut two small holes through bottle from one side to the other and string a piece of elastic through the holes with a wire. The elastic ends need to be tied to form a circle loop on each side of the bottle. You can also use an empty, clean bleach bottle for this project. Children will put an arm through each side of the bottle strap, so the bottle will stay on their back.

Long shirts or rain coats can be their fire coats. You can buy the long shirts at a thrift store. If you can't find a suitable color for them, you can buy plain white ones and dye them the color that you would like. There will be a lot of fun interaction with these props.

Be sure and have plenty of play phones for them to use. You can ask parents to save their old phones for the children to use. Also, have clip boards with pens or pencils attached too, so they can write down address for the fire fighters. This gives the opportunity for lots of expressive language that will be used while playing and learning social skills of sharing too.

## SCIENCE

Put out several bowls with a little dirt in them and paper cups with a small amount of water in them to make a slight mud. Trays will hold the bowls, cups and spoons for children to use. There will also be paper for the finger painting with the mud. Children will experiment with the materials, how they look and how they feel.

Posters and books will be on another table showing water and smoke from the fire. These items need to be kept dry. Also on this table there will color viewers to look through. Make them in several colors that the fire fighters might see at night or through the flames. To make them, use an empty card board tube from a toilet paper or towel roll. Buy colored cellophane from a craft store. Cut out a large square of cellophane and place it over one end of the tube. Then secure it with an elastic band. Next, use wide duct tape to secure all the cellophane edges by wrapping it around them. This will make it pretty durable. Make other color tubes in the same manner.

## GROSS MOTOR SKILLS

### Fire Trucks and Cars

Collect cardboard boxes from stores and put them outside. Also take out bright colors of poster paint. Children will paint the boxes and make them into cars and fire trucks. Have paper plates out so that the children can paint them black for the tires. When the paint is dry, attach the wheels to the outside bottom of the box. Put a hole in the center of each wheel and a hole through the box. Then put a fixable wire that has been folded over through the hole in the wheel and the box. Then put the wire through a washer or nut and wrap it around several times to keep the wheel in place. Next on the inside of the box spread the wire apart and use duct tape on the wires to hold them onto the box. Do the same with the rest of the wheels. Let the children use markers to draw details onto the box. For example, draw head lights and make license plates. Now put holes through two of the box sides. Put rope through the holes to make large straps for the children's arms to go though. The straps will rest on the children's shoulders. The ends of the rope need to be tied together or if the rope is thick, just tie the ends in knots and they won't pull through the cardboard.

Children are ready to have fun driving their cars around outside. Some of the children could be busy fire fighters going to put out fires, so have the pretend phones outside to call them for aid. Others could be police officers directing the traffic.

### Fire Obstacle Course

Make an obstacle course to escape the pretend fire. Have a big box open on both sides for the starting of the course. The box will represent the door to go through to exit. Have tables to crawl under and step on to go up or down along with chairs to walk around. Then have them go through the real door to the outside. When they are outside they will follow the teacher over to a safe place from the building to meet together. Then the teacher will talk about what they will do when they have a fire drill or a real emergency. Then lead the children back into the class.

## Stop, Drop, and Roll

For this activity the teacher will make a large die. On the die will be directions for the children to do. One direction will say to stop, drop and roll and another direction will say to craw low under the smoke. Other directions will be part of the fire fighter's workout routine to keep them in shape for fighting fires and helping people. The exercises will show pictures of what they will be doing, like touching their toes, hopping on one foot, turning their arms round in a circle while holding them out to the side and the last one will be marching in place. Children will take turns rolling the large die and all the children will do the exercises together. Play continues until they have all had a turn rolling the die, they are too tired or the time is over for that activity. Be sure and tell the children that you will write down the names of the children that did not have a turn, so that they will be first next time.

## FIELD TRIP IDEAS

Schedule a trip to the fire station. Prepare the children ahead of time with field trip safety reminders - like staying with the teacher or a parent. Also bring the questions that the children thought of when they did the language activity "Equipment". Another idea to do before going on the field trip would be to have the children make a special thank you card for the firefighters.

They could draw pictures of houses on fire with the fire fighters helping put it out or anything else they would like to draw about safety. When you get there, ask the fire fighters to show children various fire equipment such as ladders, hoses, special clothing, light and the alarm. It would be nice if they could also show you their exercise room and kitchen where they eat. Be sure and thank them before you leave and give them the cards that the children made them.

If you are unable to go to a fire station, ask if they could bring their truck to your school for the children to see. Ask if they could also show their special clothing and talk to them about fire safety. Be sure and make them a thank you card.

## *Special Days*

This unit uses a variety of shorter themes for short weeks with less days of school or can be used in combination with other short themes to fit your needs.

## HAT DAYS

### GROUP ACTIVITIES/CIRCLE TIME

### MUSIC AND MOVEMENT

"Wiggle Wobble" from "We all Live Together" Vol. 1 CD & tape by Greg & Steve. This is a fun song to get children moving. It also reinforces left and right sides of the body.

"My Hat It Has Three Corners" from "My Toes Are Starting To Wiggle!" tape by Miss Jackie Silberg, Distributed by: Gryphon House. This German Folk Song is fun to act out.

**My Hat It Has Three Corners**

My hat (touch you head)

It has three (put up three fingers up) Corners.

Three corners (put up three fingers)

Has my hat (touch head)

And had it not (shake index finger back and forth)

three corners (hold up three fingers)

It would not be my hat (touch head)

"My Hat" song by Sharlit Elliott with hat actions. Children should bring a hat from home to wear or the teacher will provide a hat. Song published in this book.

**My Hat** (This song is done to the tune, "The Mulberry Bush" Traditional)

This is the way we wear our hat, (Show picture of sun.)

wear our hat, wear our hat. (Pull brim of hat to shade eyes.)

This is the way we wear our hat

on a bright and sunny morning.


This is the way we wear our hat, (Show picture of stormy weather.)

wear our hat, wear our hat, (Hold hat on head, so it won't blow off.)

This is the way we wear our hat,

on a very stormy morning.


This is the way we wear our hat, (Show picture of silly faces.)

wear our hat, wear our hat, (Put hat on in a silly way.)

This is the way we wear our hat

on a silly, silly morning.


This is the way we wear our hat, (Show picture of happy faces.)

wear our hat, wear our hat, (Put a big smile on your face.)

This is the way we wear our hat

on a really, happy morning.


"Clean Up" from Barney's Favorites Vol. 1 - Traditional. This song is a great way to get the children helping to clean up the room, so that everyone will be ready for the next activity.

"My Mother Is a Baker" from "Dr. Jean & Friends" by Dr. Jean. Children enjoy doing actions to this song as talks about the different occupations that family members have.

## LANGUAGE AND LITERACY

Caps For Sale told by Esphyr Slobodkina, Scholastic Inc. 1985. Children enjoy this book. Use it several times. The first time you read the book to the children, have them tell you what happened in the book. The next time you read the book, act out the story by using real hats on your head and have the children do the monkey part with help. The next time you read it have part of the children be the peddler in the book with paper plates for hats. The other part of the children will be the monkeys. They enjoy shaking their hands and making noises as monkeys.

Hats, Hats, Hats by Ken Heyman, Scholastic Inc. 1991. This book has beautiful photographs of many different kinds of hats. Lead a discussion with the children as he/she turns each page. Bring out in the discussion that hats have many different purposes.

The Hat by Jan Brett, Scholastic Inc. 1997. This book has many beautiful pictures. Remember to turn the pages slowly, so that children can study the many things going on in the pictures. This book will also be used in a language activity at table times.

Huff and Puff's Hat Relay by Jean Warren, Warren Publishing House, 1995. This is a story book which includes 16 pages of songs and activities.

The Cat in the Hat by Dr. Seuss, Random House 1987.

Take Your Hat Off When the Flag Goes By by Janeen Brady, 1987. This book comes with a tape. It is a child's musical introduction to the constitution.

Teacher please send notes home so that parents will know about "Hat Days". Invite them to help their child find a hat or cap to wear during those days. It could be a plain hat or decorated hat. It could be a ball hat or a different type like a fireman hat or a pretty flower hat. Don't forget to discuss each of the books that you choose to read with children. They like to contribute their ideas about the stories read to them.

## SMALL GROUP ACTIVITIES/TABLE TIMES

## MATH & COGNITIVE

### Hat Counters

Draw a simple hat like the ones found in the book "Caps For Sale". Then use that for a pattern and make ten of them in different colors or on different patterns of paper. Pattern papers are often found in the dollar store in the scrapbook section. Write on each hat a numeral from 1-10. Now put small sticker such as stars on the backs of each, so that the number of stickers matches the numeral and laminate them.

Children will pick a hat and name the numeral written on it. If they can't recognize it, they will turn it over and count the stickers and say how many stickers are on it. Each child will take several turns naming numerals. Then the children will put the numerals in correct order from 1-10.

### Fish Counting

Children will use the fish bowl they made in fine motor (see below) or use a clear cup to put fish shaped crackers in. If using the fish bowl, have children take a small handful and they count how many fish there are in your hand. Now have them glue them onto the bowl while counting them to you.

Help them write the correct numeral on their fish bowl and give them a few fish crackers to eat.

If using the cup, have them take a handful of fish crackers and put them in the cup while counting them. Next they will take them out of their cup and count as they take them out. Last let them eat them.

### Baking

Teacher will make baker hats from paper like photo or purchase lunch hats from a restaurant supple store. Teacher will supply a large copy of a muffin recipe along with a box of muffin mix. Children will all take turns either adding the ingredients, mixing the muffins or putting the muffins into the paper liner cups to bake.

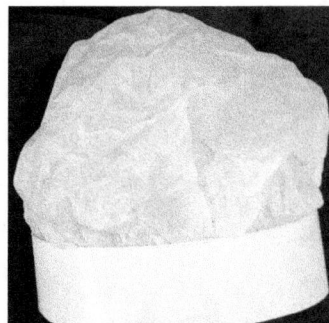

## ✂ FINE MOTOR SKILLS

### Cat in the Hat

Draw a hat like the one found in the book, "The Cat in the Hat". Make it large like the one in the picture. Then place it over 10 pieces of paper and staple once on each side of the hat and cut them out. Keep doing this until you have enough for each of the children in your class.

Set out aprons, watercolors, brushes, small cups with water in them and hats. Show the children the book with the hats in it for ideas and then tell them to paint their hats however they want.

### Fish Bowl

Draw a fish bowl like the pattern below on white or colored paper. Sometimes it is fun to put it on light blue paper so it looks like there is water inside. Let them watercolor the bowl and let it dry. Later you can use this in the counting activity or tie it in with the Cat in the Hat story.

### Newspaper Hat

Supply enough newspapers for each child to have one double sheet of paper. Demonstrate the steps to make one first, then have children follow your directions one step at a time.

Take one piece of newspaper and fold the large sheets of paper together down the middle.

Then fold the sheets in half.

Now fold from the folded end the corners. Fold them one at a time they will form rectangles. They should meet together down the middle.

Next open the other ends up and fold each side up two times or until they meet the rectangle part.

Put one staple at each end to keep rolled up

Open the hat up and wear it.

Optional - Decorate the hat with paper shapes, other items and then glue. See example.

## Baker Hats

Draw a large baker hat to use as a pattern and then cut out many at the same time by stacking paper under the pattern. Continue to cut them in this manner until you have one for each child. Now put out different shapes of noodles, sequins, various kinds of beans and glue. Tell the children to decorate their hat with the supplies anyway they want to. See example.

## Paper Plate Hat

Put out a supply of paper plates for the children. Have the children punch out two holes, one on each side of the plate. Give each child a piece of yarn about 1 1/3 yards long. They will thread the yarn from one hole to the next. This part will be used to tie the hat under their chins when the hat is completed.

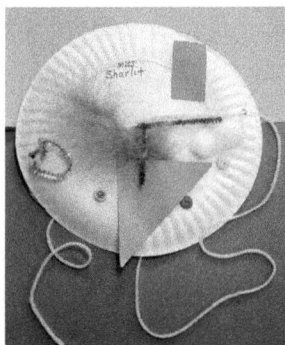

Be sure that they write their names on them.

Now set out feathers, sparkly pipe cleaners, buttons, and foam shapes. Children will choose which things they will glue onto their hats. See example.

## LANGUAGE AND LITERACY

## Hat Book

Review with the children the book "The Hat" by Jan Brett. Turn the pages slowly and ask different children to tell what is happening on the page shown. Ask the children what they think the animals thought of Hedgie and what the other animals did at the end of the story. This activity will help with expressive language and recall.

**Hat Drawing**

Children will be given markers and paper and asked to draw a picture of them self wearing their favorite kind of hat. When they finish with their picture, the teacher will ask the child about their picture. Write the child's words on their picture page. Be sure and ask the child where it's okay to write his/her words.

**Hat Game**

Obtain several different hats, such as a cowboy/cowgirl hat, fire worker hat, baseball hat, construction hat, clown hat, bike safety hat, and a baker's hat.

Teacher will play the song "My mother is a Baker" or any fun song while children pass around the same number of hats as the number of children at your table. When the music stops, the person wearing the baker hat will tell the others what he/she likes to bake or cook. (It's hard for them to know how things are cooked.)

Then the person to his/her right will tell something about the hat they are wearing. For example if he/she was wearing the fire worker hat, they would say something about their job. ("I like to save people from the fire.")

Play music again when they have all had a turn. Stop music again and the baker hat child starts saying something like "I like to make cake and eat it." This language activity is to help children use expressive language, so try and get them not to say the same thing as the last person. Continue until each child has had two or more turns.

## FREE TIME

## CREATIVE ARTS

Place large sheets of watercolor paper on the easel. Also put out stamps, stamp pads and markers. Make sure that the stamp pad has washable ink in it. Let the children create anything that they want. It is a good idea to use a piece of yarn tied to a pen and the other end of it tied to each side of the easel. This way the children can practice writing their own names. You can help them if they need help writing their name.

## SENSORY

Use flour in the table with bowls, spoons, sifters, mini size muffin tins and mini bread pans. Children will enjoy this activity, but set the rules before they play there so there isn't too big of a mess.

## DRAMATIC PLAY & SOCIAL DEVELOPMENT

Provide a prop box with lots of different kinds of hats that they can wear. Be sure and have a mirror close by for them to see themselves.

## SCIENCE

Place an assortment of items that will attract magnets and a few other items that will not be attracted to them. Also, have books about magnets at the table along with picture books showing different hats. Pick these books up at your local library. You can find them in the nonfiction section for children.

## GROSS MOTOR SKILLS

Play the game "Duck, Duck, Goose". Use the words Hat, Hat, Boot in place of the other words. The children set on the floor in a circle with one child being "it". That child goes around the outside of the circle while saying, "Hat, Hat" until he/she reaches the person that he/she wants to chase him/her. Then he/she says "Boot" and that child gets up and runs around the circle after the "it" person. The "it" person tries to be sitting in the other child's space that is chasing him before the other person gets there. Then the other child that was chasing them, is "it". The "it" person repeats what the 1st child did, but picks a child that hasn't had a turn. Play continues in this manner until all children have had at least one turn.

### Marching

Children will wear their newspaper hats that were made at the fine motor activity. Then they will march around the room. Use the song "I'm a V. I. P." by Janeen Brady or "Hurray For the World" from "Teaching Peace" CD by Red Grammer.

## FIELD TRIP IDEAS

If you live in an area that has a clothing or pioneer museum, make arrangements to visit there. Children may be surprised to see that people have been wearing hats for many years. Talk about the purposes that the hats had, such as the pioneer bonnets helped to protect them from the sun and wind. Also the hats with the wide brim, now called cowboy/cowgirl hats helped to protect them from the sun and storms.

# SHOES & SOCKS

### Teacher Instructions to Involve Parents

Send a parent note home before this day so that parents can help the children find special socks to wear on this day or more days. Tell the parents that the socks could be decorated socks or have a design or pattern that the child really likes or they could be funny. Funny ones might be designed or mismatched ones. Let them have fun planning them. Then on the special day(s) have each child show their socks to the other children in their class.

## GROUP ACTIVITIES/CIRCLE TIME

### MUSIC AND MOVEMENT

"Those Magic Shoes!" from Macmillian Sing & Learn Program by Newbridge Communications, Inc. In this song children make believe that they have magic shoes that can turn them into an astronaut, a lion tamer and a rock-and-roll star.

"The Side Step" from Macmillian Sing & Learn Program by Newbridge Communications, Inc.

In this song, children follow directions of stepping to the right and to the left while learning to dance.

"One, Two, Buckle My Shoe" from "We Sing Grandpa's Magical Toys" tape. This song is fun for the children to act out.

"Oh Hey Oh Hi Hello" from "Jim Gill Makes It Noisy In Boise, Idaho" by Jim Gill. Children use their voices to be soft, loud, sad, angry and even sound like they are singing under water in this fun song.

"Introduction To Crazy Shoes Theme" by Jill Gill from "Moving Rhymes for Modern Times."

"Crazy Shoes Theme" by Jill Gill from "Moving Rhymes for Modern Times."

## LANGUAGE AND LITERACY

First read the book, <u>A Pair of Socks</u> by Stuart J. Murphy, Scholastic, Inc. 1996. Then have the children look at the pages again and ask them questions about what they see. Use this book to help children learn about matching colors and patterns. Next ask the children to look at their own socks and tell the class what their socks look like.

When each child has had a turn describing their socks, help them to see similarities and differences in their socks. They will group them according to what they find such as plain colors, stripes, patterns and picture type. Have them sit by others with the same similarities.

Then draw a picture of the general types at the top of a large wipe off board and make columns down from them. Next they will take turns selecting which column their socks belong. They will write an "X" on that column.

When each person has finished looking at the graph, have the children determine which has the most and the least by looking at how long the columns are. Next have them count each column roll to determine the largest number and the smallest number of similar socks. Make sure that you tell them are their socks are great and it doesn't matter if there are lots or few socks like theirs. All the socks cover their feet and keep them warm and that some types of shoes don't need socks to be worn with them.

The following are also great books for this unit:

<u>Socks for Supper</u> by Jack Kent, Parents' Magazine Press, 1978. This book is about a poor couple that exchange socks for cheese and milk and they receive more than they expected.

<u>Who Uses This</u>? by Margaret Miller, Scholastic, Inc. 1990. As children listen to the story, have them pay special attention to the pictures so that see what the people are wearing on their feet.

<u>All About Things People Do</u> by Lesley Smith, Scholastic, Inc. 1989. This book shows more people with different vocations and the types of shoes they wear. Ask children what job their mom and dad do and what kinds of shoes they wear.

Froggy Gets Dressed by Jonathan London, Scholastic, Inc. 1992. This book helps to show children that socks and boots help to keep your feet warm in the winter.

Mrs. Toggle's Beautiful Blue Shoe by Robin Pulver, Trumpet, 1997. This is a fun story about a teacher that lost one of her beautiful blue shoes.

The Children That Lived In A Shoe by Josephine Van Dolzen Pease, Rand McNally & Company.

Children will really enjoy these books. It would be nice to send a note listing the books you will be reading or that you would like parents to read to their children. Also, don't forget to let parents know about "shoe day". Parents could let children wear shoes that are different, like dance shoes, cowboy boots, slippers or dress shoes. Then on "shoe day" have children stand in the center of your circle to show their shoes off. Be sure and wear something different yourself on your feet.

## SMALL GROUP ACTIVITIES/TABLE TIMES

### MATH & COGNITIVE

Use memory match cards from "The Education Center, Inc." Dec./Jan.2003-4 book. They have a large selection of different types of shoes. Or, if you don't have access to that or can't find it, you can make your own. Color and copy them to make a memory match game or cut out pictures of different shoes from magazines and mount them on cards. Then have color copies made of them to use and have them laminated.

At first, have children take turns matching the cards face up. Then the next time they play have the cards turned face down. Have the children draw three cards to see if they can make a match. If no matches have been made, have them return the cards to the same spot that they took them turning them face down. Have children pay attention to where they put them, so that they can make matches later. The next child takes a turn and if they make a match they take another turn until they miss making a match. Play continues until all the cards have been matched. Then each child will count how many cards that they matched. Don't say that there is a winner, just comment on that they did a good job counting and matching.

## Shoe Puzzles

Go to a school supply store to buy puzzles. If you can't find the shoe puzzle, buy one of the puzzles that shows children dressed in seasonal clothing or any puzzle that you think would work. Set out the new puzzle with the other puzzles that you already have.

## Dot to Dot Shoe

Make a simple pattern of a shoe and then erase parts of the shoe and add numbers with a dot. Children will find the number 1 dot and connect it to the number 2 dot and so on until all the dots have been connected. Don't use many too many numbers, at the most use 10 numbers so it won't be too hard for them to do. See example.

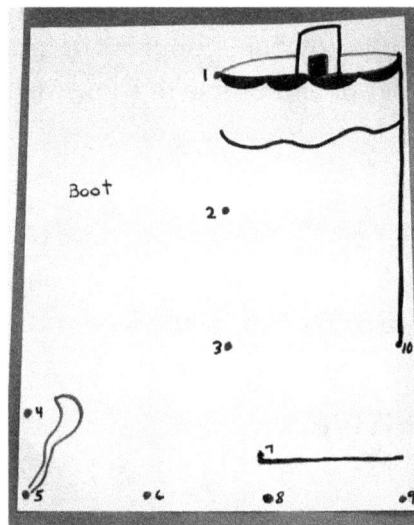

## ✂ FINE MOTOR SKILLS

## Shoe Tracing

1. Make a pattern of a cowboy/cowgirl boot. Then, cut out several patterns on heavy weight paper. The children will use these patterns to trace their own boot and cut it out. Save these boots for the next day.

2. Children will use the boot shape that they cut out to collage decorations on. Teacher will provide beads, small colored wood shapes (found at the dollar store) and sequins to glue on their boot.

## Lacing Shoe

Provide real laced shoes for the children to learn to lace on or provide colorful foam shoes shapes for children to practicing lacing. You can find shoes that lace at the thrift store or ask parents to donate lace shoes that are no longer needed at their house.

If you choose to do the foam ones, draw one that look like the example on paper and then trace it onto the foam. Then make four or five more. Punch holes in the shoe for the laces to go through. Buy shoe laces to go through each child's shoe (found at the dollar store). Now demonstrate how to cross the laces over to make an "X". Let them practice lacing several times.

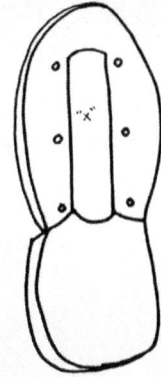

## Children That Lived In A Shoe

Draw a tall large shoe house and make enough copies for each child. Then read the story The Children That Lived In A Shoe and give each of the children a copy of the shoe

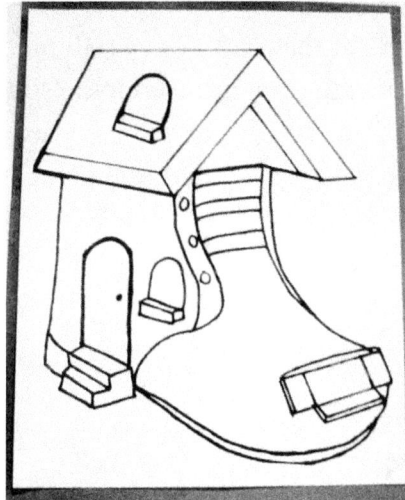

house. Children will draw with markers the children that lived in the shoe. They will also draw the grass and other things that they would like to be by their house. See pattern.

## LANGUAGE AND LITERACY

### Shoe Patterning

Use a die cut of a shoe to make shoes in three or four different colors. If you do not have a die cut available, use stickers with circle smiley faces on them in three or four colors. Make one long 2 ½ inch strip for each child to place their patterns on.

Now the teacher will demonstrate by making a pattern with the materials and either glue them on the strip or pull off the stickers and placing them in a pattern on the strip. Next, the children will each make a pattern on their own strip. Children will show you their patterns when they are finished and also tell you the colors that they used to make their pattern.

### Singing a Song

Children will listen to song, "One, Two, Buckle My Shoe" from "We Sing Grandpa's Magical Toys" that was sang early at the circle. They will practice the song and learn to do the movements. The movements are: pretend to buckle shoes, pretend to shut the door, pretend to pick up sticks, lay them straight, be a big fat hen by bending both arms at the elbow and bouncing them up and down by making a clucking sound.

## FREE TIME

## CREATIVE ARTS

Put colored paper out on the easel with colored chalk and let them create whatever they want.

## SENSORY

Put packing peanuts in the table with little people to hide and play.

Let the children play with small dolls in the table with shoes for them to wear.

## DRAMATIC PLAY & SOCIAL DEVELOPMENT

Go to shoe stores to ask for some old shoe advertisement posters. Use the posters to decorate that part of your room where you feature dramatic play. This area will be your pretend shoe store. Have lots of different types of shoes on hand for the children to try on and to wear. Put a ruler or two out for children to measure their feet. Also, place toy phones, cash registers, play money, bags to put shoes and small clip boards with paper and pencil on them to write up their order. Then let the children name the store and write up the name on a piece of poster board. Children will take turns being the clerk and the customer.

## SCIENCE

On the science table, place kaleidoscopes, bottles with colored water mixed with oil to shake and observe. Also include bottles with colored water and small objects in them. Some of the items could be light like sequins and some could be heavy like marbles. Add one more bottle with corn syrup in it and heavy objects like marbles and steel balls. These items will have the children exploring and trying to figure things out.

## GROSS MOTOR SKILLS

Take the children outside to play follow the leader. The leader will use directions like run behind me, cross your feet and hop, walk fast and move your arms up and down to fly and kick your legs high. Then let a child be the leader for a short time. Keep track of who has been the leader, so that on another day others can take their turn.

Use chalk to draw shapes on the sidewalk such as - squares, circles, triangles and rectangles. Then when he/she says the name of two shapes as many children as possible will try to walk and stand inside those shapes. Next time, the teacher will say two different shapes and the children will tip toe to those shapes. The teacher will continue to name two shapes and give different directions on how to get there. Play continues until children are starting to get tired.

Have the children play "toss the socks". Ask parents to send in old clean socks for this activity. Have children match up the socks that are the same length and then roll them together. Then help them tuck the cuff over the rolled one. Now put a laundry basket inside a circle and have children stay behind the circle to throw the socks into the basket. Have one child from each side throw at the same time and then they will pick up the socks and give them to the next two people to throw.

## FIELD TRIP IDEAS

On this field trip you will visit a local shoe store. The teacher will make a lotto card before going on this field trip for each child. Make the card by making three columns down and three columns across. Now cut out many different kinds of shoes from advertisements. Make sure that the pictures used for the card show the type of shoes that the children will be seeing at the shoe store.

Next, paste the pictures inside each of the squares on the card. Now go to the copy store and have one copied for each child. Keep a master. You can make the cards disposable after their use or permanent by laminating them. Take watercolor markers for the children to mark their cards.

Tell the children that they will be going on a field trip and that they will be seeing many different kinds of shoes.

Show them the prepared cards and explain to them that, they will be taking marker with them. When they see the same kind of shoe that is on their card they will put an "X" through it. Tell them to look for all the kinds of shoes on their card.

Remind them of the safety rules and good manners to use. Also take a card to thank the store for letting you come.

# BACKWARDS/OPPOSITE

## GROUP ACTIVITIES/CIRCLE TIME

### MUSIC AND MOVEMENT

"Good Morning" from Macmillian Sing & Learn Program by Newbridge Communications, Inc. This is a song with a strong beat that makes you feel good. You can sing this with both your afternoon and morning classes. Sing this song with the afternoon class and then change the words in the song from good morning to good afternoon and sing the rest of the words the same as before. This will have your children why you are sing the wrong time of day. Remind them that it is backwards day.

"Opposites" from Macmillian Sing & Learn Program by Newbridge Communications, Inc. This song is a fun way for children to learn what opposite means while doing actions that are opposite from each other, such as right, left and yes, no.

"Over, Under" from Macmillian Sing & Learn Program by Newbridge Communications, Inc. Children act out this song using a partner. They follow direction like hands go over, hands go under.

"The Q and A Song" from Macmillian Sing & Learn Program by Newbridge Communications, Inc. Children need lots of practicing understanding what is opposite and this song helps with it. An example is when the question in the song says "what is the opposite of up?" In the song the children's voices answers with "down."

"Inside, Outside" from Macmillian Sing & Learn Program by Newbridge Communications, Inc. This is another great song that helps children learn opposites.

"Near or Far?" from Macmillian Sing & Learn Program by Newbridge Communications, Inc. This song helps with the concepts what is near and what is far.

"High, Low" from Macmillian Sing & Learn Program by Newbridge Communications, Inc. This is a song about a giraffe and a worm.

"Backwards Day" by Jim Gill from CD, "Jim Gill Sings Moving Rhymes for Modern Times." This song talks about a backwards day.

"Opposites" by Dr. Jean, from "Ole! Ole! Ole! Dr. Jean en Español" CD. This song is in English and the next song on the CD is the same song sung in Spanish.

"Song About Slow, Song About Fast" by Hap Palmer from "Walter the Waltzing Worm," tape. Children listen to the slow and fast tempos and do movements to the two different tempos.

"All the Ways of Jumping Up and Down" by Hap Palmer from "Walter the Waltzing Worm," tape. This is a lively song to reinforce opposites with movement and vocabulary words.

"Surprise Song" by Hap Palmer from "Walter the Waltzing Worm," tape. This song is made up of seven musical sections where children listen and follow directions such as go high, go low and move in straight paths move in curved paths.

"Up and Down A Mountain" by Hap Palmer from "Sally the Swinging Snake" tape. This song will keep children busy with many movements.

"Loud n' Soft" from "Rhythm Makers" Tom Thumb. This tape uses clapping, your voices and or instrument to teach loud and soft sound concepts.

## LANGUAGE AND LITERACY

Opposites Consultant Ph.D. Istar Schwager, Publications International Ltd. 1994.

What's Opposite? by Stephen R. Swinburne, Boyds Troll 2000.

A Push 'N' Pull Book of Opposites by Graham Brown, Scholastic Inc. 1992.

Inside Outside Upside Down by Stan and Jan Berenstain, Random House/New York 1968.

Big and Small, Short and Tall by Muriel Batherman, Scholastic Inc. 1972.

Left or Right? By Karl Rehm and Kay Koike, Scholastic Inc. 1993.

Big Sister and Little Sister by Charlotte Zolotow, Harper & Row, Publishers 1966.

The Puppy Who Wanted a Boy by Jane Thayer, William Morrow & Company, Inc. 1985.

Outside and Inside You by Sandra Markle, Scholastic Inc. 1991.

What's Inside? My Body by A. Dorling Kindersly Book, Scholastic Inc 1991.

What's Inside? Toys by A. Dorling Kindersly Book, Scholastic Inc 1991.

These books have great photos and/or pictures. Some of the books have a simple introduction to the subject example – What's Opposite? Read this book slowly and have children look carefully look at the photos. As the book progresses, the author asks questions. Have the children in your class take turns answering them. Then when you're through reading, ask the children to think of some other things that have opposites. Have children take turns naming the two opposite items they thought of.

Another day read The Puppy Who Wanted a Boy. Then have the children think how his story could have an opposite. Then have them tell their favorite part of the story.

Be sure and sent a note to parents about "opposite or backwards days," so that children can wear parts of their clothing backwards those days. They could wear their shirt, skirt, belt, hat or sweater backwards that day.

Also, ask parents to help you teach about opposites by showing things around their house that have opposites. You can also greet the children backwards by saying "Morning Good" and "Afternoon Good". If possible, rearrange the order of the things you do to be backwards too. Don't forget to wear something backwards too.

## SMALL GROUP ACTIVITIES/TABLE TIMES

### MATH & COGNITIVE

**Number Cards**

Buy a deck or number cards at the Dollar store or make your own. Use plain index cards and write numerals 1-20 on them. Add small stickers or shapes on each card with the same amount of shapes as the numeral on it.

Spread out the cards on the table and have the children arrange them in order from 1-10 or 1-20 depending on the abilities of the children in your class. Next have them arrange the cards backwards with the largest first and the least last. Now count them together backwards.

**Play Dough Shapes**

Make the play dough recipe found in this book in the theme Pajamas & Monsters under Fine Motor.

Add a little sparkle to the dough by putting glitter in with the flour when making it. Also make shape cards for the children to use as examples.

Now place examples of shapes such as a square, circle, heart, diamond, triangle and rectangle on the table. Have children make each of the shapes with their play dough. Before leaving the table each child will tell the names of the shapes and point to them that they made. If they need help naming them, have child with your help names each of the shapes again.

## Order Clothing

Make a simple pattern of a hat, a shirt, a skirt and a pair of pants. See example. Now use your pattern to make four more sets of them and laminate them to use at your table with the children.

Children will correctly order the clothing from largest to smallest. Then teach them to state ordinal positions of the objects (1st, 2nd, 3rd, and 4th Position).

## FINE MOTOR SKILLS

### Under Table Drawings

Put large pieces of butcher paper under tables and tape it there. When children come to the table, have them pick crayons or markers to use. Then they will lie on their backs under the table and draw a picture. After everyone has drawn put the paper up in the class, so everyone can see their art work.

### Face Opposites

Make a simple head pattern such as the example. Then use that pattern to trace off on to poster paper to make patterns for the children to use. Now gather child sized scissors, construction paper, pencils, crayons, markers and glue.

Children will use the pattern head to trace onto a piece of construction paper that has been folded in half. Then they will cut out the head while keeping the paper folded to produce two heads. Children will glue the two heads onto a full sheet of paper.

Now tell them to think of opposite feelings. Tell the teacher what the two opposites are and teacher will write the opposites on their paper with one over each picture or use small printed faces to draw or glue onto the page. Example happy/sad. Children will draw faces on each head to represent each emotion that they named.

## Cake Cones

This fun activity has something to bake in a hot oven used to cook but, uses a cold ice cream cone to cook it in. Buy a cake mix and the ingredients to make it. She/he will also buy a can of whipping cream and a package of ice cream cones with flat bottoms.

Children will prepare the cake mix by following the directions on the box. Then they will take turns spooning batter into the cones until the cone is about ¾ full. Then they will put their cone into a muffin pan. Teacher will have the oven preheated to 350 degrees. Teacher will put the muffin pan into the oven and cook it for about 30 minutes. Check to make sure it is done with a toothpick. When it's done set it on a cooling rack. When it has cooled let the children each squirt the top with the whipping cream and enjoy their treat.

## LANGUAGE AND LITERACY

### Opposite Collage

Provide construction paper that has been cut down the middle two pieces for each child and glue. Also provide things that are hard such as beads, beans, colored noodles and things that are soft such as cotton balls, pieces of soft material and feathers.

Children will discuss the materials at the table and categorize them into two groups. Tell children that these two groups are not the same. Ask how they are different from each other. Ask how they are opposite from each other. Now have each child make a picture that is opposite from the other picture.

### My Opposite Book

Ask parents to help supply old magazines for children to cut. Set out construction paper that has been folded in half and stapled to form a book. Also have ready for use scissors and glue.

Children will find pictures to cut out that show opposites. An example would be a child standing and another one of a child sitting. Once the pictures are selected, the children glue the two pictures next to each other in their book. The child will tell the teacher the words to write on each page of their book.

### Backwards Story

Use pictures of things that are familiar to children. Then mount the pictures to make a set of three or four pictures that could tell a short story. An example would be a picture of a baby, a toddler, a preschool aged child and a grade school aged picture. Make a few sets and then set the sets out one as a time and have children tell a story using the cards in the correct order. Then have the children take turns telling the story backwards. Next proceed to the next set of cards and follow the same procedure.

## FREE TIME

### CREATIVE ARTS

Have large sheets of water color paper on the easel and poster paint mixed in cups ready in several colors. Tell children that today is a special day so they will do their painting with their opposite hand today. Remind them what opposite means. If they normally paint with their right hand then the opposite hand would be to use their left hand.

### SENSORY

Fill the sensory table with warm water and have farm animals in the tube to swim for opposite day or put sand in the table and put plastic fish to swim in the sand.

### DRAMATIC PLAY & SOCIAL DEVELOPMENT

Teacher will put out a box of dress up clothing with hats, ties, shoes and jewelry assessors to go along with the clothing. Encourage the children to take turns with the clothing. Also provide a large mirror so that the children can see how they look and lots on telephones so that they can call each other. Other items that would be helpful for their play would be a small table and chairs, pretend stove, sink, cupboard, fridge, pretend food and baby dolls.

## SCIENCE

Put out the books <u>What's Inside? My Body</u> and <u>What's Inside? Toys</u>. Then put out an old stuffed animal and have it undone or cut open so that they can what is inside it. Also put out any non-working item such as a clock that they can take apart to examine. Be sure to include screw drivers in various sizes or any other tools that will help them to take it apart.

## GROSS MOTOR SKILLS

**Backwards Game**

Prepare index cards by writing gross motor movements such as hopping on one foot, jumping with both feet, spinning around, walking backwards, and tiptoeing. Then she/he will acquire a large die or make one from a school milk carton.

Children will sit in a circle until it is their turn. Then the child whose turn it is will stand and go to the middle of the circle. Next the child will pick a movement index card from the floor. The teacher says what the words are on the card and the child will shake the die to see how many times to do the movement.

The children will count the dots on the die to see how many times to do the activity. They will all stand up in their circle and do the activity that many times, but this will be tricky to do because they will all count backward to do it. An example would be to hop on one foot 5 times. They would counted 5, 4, 3, 2, 1 and then stop.

The next child would come forward. Play will continue until all children have had a turn drawing a card and the shaking the die.

If you don't have enough time to finish the game, record on a piece of paper who still needs a turn and tell them that they will get a turn on the next day.

### Follow the Leader

Take the children out side and play follow the leader. The teacher will be the 1st leader. She/he will say what she/he is doing and do the movement and the children will follow in a line and do the same movement. Movements can include tiptoe, skip, skate, hop walk backwards, dance, fly, gallop, spin, walk on all fours, swim and jog. Another day the teacher will choose different children to each be the leaders for short time.

## FIELD TRIP IDEAS

Children will go on a walking trip around the block. First they will walk forward and then they will turn around and walk carefully, looking over their backs, backwards. Then when teacher directs they will turn around again and walk forward again. The time that they walk backwards should only be for a short time and forward should be the longest time. When they get back, ask the children which way was the best way to walk and why they though so. Then vote on which way was their favorite. They can only vote one way. If it was forward have their hand on their head and if backward their hand should be on their back. Count both ways and see which had most votes.

## *Pajamas & Monsters*

## GROUP ACTIVITIES/CIRCLE TIME

## MUSIC AND MOVEMENT

"Five Little Monsters" from Macmillian Sing & Learn Program by Newbridge Communications, Inc. In this song the children take turns pretending to be a monster outside a door knocking on it. A boy or girl follows the directions in the song. Then at the end he or she opens it for a big surprise.

"Sleeping Time" from Macmillian Sing & Learn Program by Newbridge Communications, Inc. Children sing this song on the day that they wear their pajamas to school. They have fun pretending.

"Walking to the ABCs" from Macmillian Sing & Learn Program by Newbridge Communications, Inc. This is a fun song to do that helps children get their wiggles out while helping them learn to follow directions and learn their letters.

"Moon Play" from Macmillian Sing & Learn Program by Newbridge Communications Inc. This song helps children to learn about the moon's different shapes that they see at night.

"Use Your Imagination" from Macmillian Sing & Learn Program by Newbridge Communications, Inc. This song helps them to learn the difference between make believe and real. It's ok to make believe, but you need to know the difference between them.

"Yellow Marshmallow" from Macmillian Sing & Learn Program by Newbridge Communications, Inc. This is a fun song to act out while you pretend and be a yellow eyed monster.

"The Scary Song" from Macmillian Sing & Learn Program by Newbridge Communications, Inc. This is a fun song that helps them laugh at monsters and ghosts.

"Mean Words" from Macmillian Sing & Learn Program by Newbridge Communications, Inc. This song teaches that it hurts others when you say mean words. You can make a mean-words monster and put it on the front of a jar and what the mean words that teacher or children hear in class, write on a paper and put inside the jar and not say them anymore.

"A Favorite Thing" from Macmillian Sing & Learn Program by Newbridge Communications, Inc. Have the children in your class bring to school their favorite stuffed animal that sleeps on their bed. Have the children hold their special animal while they sing this song.

"Tiptoeing, Tiptoeing" from Macmillian Sing & Learn Program by Newbridge Communications, Inc. This is a fun song to quiet your class down and get them to practice tiptoeing.

"Me and My Teddy" by Phillip A. Parker from "Barney's Favorites," Vol. 1 This is another fun song to use with children's stuffed animals.

"Jim Gill's Lullaby," by Jim Gill, from CD "Jim Gill Makes It Noisy in Boise, Idaho"

"Pajamas" by Livingston Taylor, from Inmmony, A Sesame Street Record.

"Imagination Communication" from "Tony Chestnut & Fun Time Action Song", The Learning Station.

"Six on the Bed" from "Here We Go Loopty Loo," The Learning Station.

## LANGUAGE AND LITERACY

Franklin's Blanket by Paulette Bourgeois, Brenda Clark, Scholastic, Inc. 1995.

I Don't Want to Go to Bed by Julie Sykes,  Scholastic, Inc. 1997.

Froggy Goes to Bed by Jonathan London, Scholastic, Inc. 2000.

Ira Sleep Over by Bernard Waber, Houghton Mifflin Company, Boston 1972.

Best Friends Sleep Over by Jacqueline Rogers, Scholastic, Inc. 1993.

No Jumping on the Bed by Tedd Arnold, Scholastic, Inc. 1994.

What Was That! By Geda Bradley Mathews, Golden Press Western Publishing Company, Inc. 1977.

Good Night Moon by Margaret Wise Brown, Harper & Row, Publishing, Inc.

Count the Ways, Little Bear by Jonathan London, Puffin Books, 2002.

How Do Dinosaurs Say Good Night? By Jane Yolen, Scholastic Inc. 2000.

The books above all are good books to read on pajama day. Froggy Goes to Bed is one of my favorites. Parents and children really relate to this story. After reading it, let the children take turns telling what they do before going to bed.

The following book list introduces monsters. Children sometimes think about these types of things before going to bed. The books listed next will help children see that monsters are really a part of our imagination. The books can also help children see the difference between imagination and real events if you take time to discuss the book in those terms with the children.

There's An Alligator Under My Bed by Mercer Mayer, Troll Associates 1987.

There's A Nightmare In My Closet by Mercer Mayer, Dial Books for Young Readers 1976.

There's Something In My Attic by Mercer Mayer, Troll Associates 1988.

Go Away, Big Green Monster! By Ed Emberley, Scholastic, Inc. 1992.

Five Ugly Monsters by Tedd Arnold, Scholastic, Inc. 1995.

Huggly and The Toy Monster by Tedd Arnold, Scholastic, Inc. 1998.

One Hungry Monster by Tedd Arnold, Scholastic, Inc. 1989.

Where The Wild Things Are by Maurice Sendak, Scholastic, Inc. 1968.

## SMALL GROUP ACTIVITIES/TABLE TIMES

## MATH AND COGNITIVE

### Counting Sheep

Use a coloring book or a die cut to find a picture of a sheep. Make copies of the sheep and write numbers on them. Have dots on the backs or stickers to represent the numbers written on the front of the sheep.

Children will take turns counting them. Only make either 1-5 or 1-10 if your class is ready go a little higher. Don't let those children fall asleep while counting them.

## Teddy Bear Match Ups

Prepare picture matching cards by drawing a small bear. Then make copies of the bear 16 times on colored construction paper. Then put shapes on the bear's tummy. Do this by cutting out and gluing two matching shapes on the bears. Then each bear will have a matching shape. Good shapes to do would be: squares, circles, triangles, rectangles, stars, hearts, ovals and crescent.

## Ten In A Bed

Children will learn the traditional song "Ten in a Bed". Teacher will provide a king or queen size blanket for this activity. Lay the blanket on the floor and have ten (or you can use less) children lay on the blanket. If you have fewer children in your group, just start the song with however many children will be in your group.

Now sing the song and when the children get to the part "roll over" the children all roll over to the same side and one rolls out. Children will count the number of children left and sing again until no one is left. Sing the song as many times as you and the children like.

### Ten In A Bed

There was ten in the bed

and a little one said

Roll over roll over

I'm crowded,

so they all rolled over

and one fell out.


There was nine in the bed - then 8,7,6,5,4,3,2,1

Continue song in same manner until you reach one.

There was one in the bed

and the little one said

I'm lonely, I'm lonely

so they all came back!

## Monster Math

Draw and cut out ten monsters and laminate them. Now, the children will count all the monsters. Then tell children to close their eyes and the teacher will hide a few. Now children will open their eyes and guess if all the monsters are there. Next they will count how many monsters are there. Now help them count to 10 again and have them put up a finger when all the monsters on the table have been counted, but we haven't reached the number ten. So, if I hide two monsters they would count the eight on the table. Then they would put up one finger for the number nine and one more finger up for the number ten. Next have them count the amount of fingers they have up, so I hide two monsters. Continue with the game as long as they are interested. If the amount is too hard for your group, use fewer monsters to count.

## Monster Pizza

This fun cooking activity will supply a healthy dose of cognitive skills. Buy tube biscuits found in the grocery store refrigerator section. Buy enough cans so that each child will have his/her own biscuit. Also buy bottled pizza sauce, pepperoni slices, olives, shredded cheese and green bell peppers.

Cover a cookie sheet with foil and section it off into squares with masking tape. These squares will be labeled with each child's name for their pizza. Have the children wash their hands before doing this activity. Give each child a biscuit and show them how to flatten it into a large circle. Then have them spread pizza sauce over it and use the pepperoni, olives, cheese and pepper to create a face on it. They could use the pepperoni to make a few eyes, the olives to make noses and they can use plastic knives to the pepper into large zigzag teeth to add on to it. The cheese can be its fur.

Have them put their pizzas on the foil by their names. Have the oven preheated before you start this activity so they won't have to wait as long. While it's cooking, ask them what they think will happen to the cheese when it's in the oven. Also talk about what might happen to the biscuit's size, shape and height. When it's cooked, compare it to what they thought would happen and ask them to guess why it did or didn't turn out the way that they thought. Then tell them to enjoy eating it.

## Dot to Dot Teddy Bear

Draw with a pencil a picture like the example or find one to enlarge from a coloring book. On the outside lines of the bear's body make numbers 1-10 with spaces in-between. Now erase the lines between the dots or use white-out to erase the lines between the numbers. This will be your pattern, so copy it on a copy machine as many times as needed for your class. The children will each receive a copy of it and also a marker or pencil to connect the dots. If they need help with number order, provide a number line on the table from 1-10 to look at.

## FINE MOTOR SKILLS

Read the book Go Away, Big Green Monster! By Ed Emberly at circle time and then follow up with this activity. Use the cut-out pages in the book to make patterns for the monsters face. After making patterns of the different parts of the face transfer them to poster board and make 4 or more pattern of each part.

Show the book to the children at the table and tell them that they will be making their own monster. Set out pencils, different colors of construction paper, child sized scissors and glue for the children's use. Explain to the children that they will trace the different parts of the face on to different colors of construction paper. They will choose the colors that they want to make their monster. Next they cut out the pieces and glue them to a paper to form their monster face. This will be not only a good fine motor activity, but also a great activity to practice following directions. Help them with directions if they need it.

### Nightmare in My Closet

Cut brown construction paper in half. This will represent the closet door. You will need one for each child in the class. Then mount it on a piece of white construction paper by stapling it along one side as in the example. Type up the words, "There's a Nightmare in My Closet" and use copy and paste on your computer until you have the amount needed for your class. Then cut the lines apart for the children to glue onto their pictures.

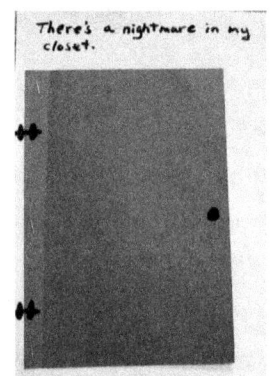

There's a nightmare in my closet.

The children will each receive a prepared sheet. They will bend open their door and draw a monster behind their door with markers. Next they will glue on the word strip. Finally, they will take this picture with them to the language table where they will use it next.

## Monster Collage

Prepare a large monster shape on poster board. Then trace out the pattern on the top of five or six pieces of colored construction paper. Continue doing this until you have enough for each child in the class. Make sure that you put out many different colors so that the children will have a choice of color for their monster.

The children will come to the table and glue different collage materials onto their monster. You can set out wiggle eyes, buttons, beans, different shapes of noodles and beads for them to choose from. See example.

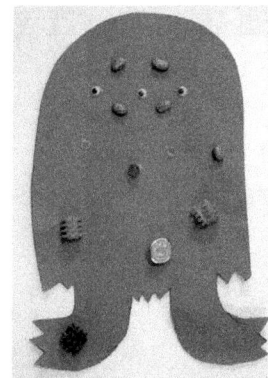

## Stars

Prepare patterns of large stars. Children will trace around the star pattern and cut it out. Then they will write their name on it with a marker. Next they will use a small bottle of glue to make a line around the edges of the star shape. Now they will set the star on a tray and sprinkle glitter on top of the glue. Last they will dump the excess glitter onto the tray and leave it on the counter to dry.

The star would be fun to hang in your class room from the ceiling. Just put a thumb tack with fishing line hooked to it on the ceiling and then have the other end of the line tied to a large paperclip from which you clip the star.

## Self-Hardening Play Dough Monsters

Make salt dough in bright colors. Then tell children to make a monster from it with lots of body parts. Have wiggle eyes that they can press into the dough. Give each child a paper plate to write their name on. When their monster is finished have them set their monster to dry on their plate.

<u>Self-Hardening Play Dough</u>

4 cups flour
1-1/2 cups salt
1 tsp. alum
*Optional 2-3 Tbs. food coloring

Mix the flour, salt and alum together. Then add the water to it gradually.*

If you want mixture colored, add coloring to water Before stirring into the flour for a smooth color. [Hint: The water needs to be very dark or the color will be very light when mixed.]

Stir to form a ball in bowl. Add more water it won't Hold together. Next knead dough. Place in a sealed Container until ready to use. After shapes have been Made leave to dry. All these ingredients can be found in the baking/spice aisle of the grocery store.

## Sheep

Draw the shape of sheep and trace the pattern. Then trace the sheep pattern on top of 5 or 6 sheets of white construction paper. Staple once on each side and cut them out. Continue cutting sheep until you have one for each child. Have the sheep cut outs, markers, glue and cotton balls for children to use.

Children will pull cotton balls to make them larger and fluffy and glue them onto their sheep. Then use markers to draw on face features.

## LANGUAGE AND LITERACY

## What Goes Together

Collect articles that children might use before going to bed. The children will then find items that go together such as a wash cloth/towel, toothbrush/toothpaste, blanket (small size)/sheet, hair brush/comb, P.J. top/P.J. bottom, bubbles/bar soap, shampoo/conditioner, and a story-book/glass of water.

Teacher will mix up the sets of items and set them on the table. Then he/she will have the children take turns naming each item. Next the teacher will have children take turns picking an item and finding something that goes with the item. Now the child will tell how the items go together. If the answer is logical accept the answer. Teacher will also tell children, that there may be more than one way to match the items together. Continuing taking turns until all the items have been mentioned in one way that might be matched to another one.

## Brown Monster, Brown Monster

Make Monsters in basic and secondary colors and tape them to a stick.

Children will sing the turn of "Brown Bear" - Traditional, with the new words to song "Brown Monster." Each child will have at least one monster stick puppet. When the teacher sings a color the child holding that stick puppet up will hold it up. The song will continue until all the color monsters have been help up. Sing the song again, but first have the children trade puppet monsters. Example below.

> Brown monster, brown monster what do you see?
>
> I see a yellow monster looking at me.
>
> Yellow monster, yellow monster what to you see?
>
> I see a green monster looking at me.

Continue with each color until you have used the last one. Then say last bears color name and then say I see many colored monsters looking at me.

## Bear Spy

Cut out small pictures from magazines of common things that children should be acquainted with such as a car, a house, a dog, a cat, a bike, a toy, a fruit, a vegetable or a dessert. Mount your pictures on white index cards and laminate them. Then use a bear pattern such as the example below.

Cut a square window in the bear. Then cut a piece of plastic the size of the hole plus a little wider. Next, use clear tape to tape around the edges on the back side of the bear. Now cut a square of brown construction paper and put it behind the clear window to form a pocket. Tape around the edges, but not the top. In this pocket you will put the picture cards you have prepared with the pictures showing.

The bear will face the teacher at first. The teacher will say can you guess what I spy?

She/he will then say:

It is_____ color,

It is a _____ (animal, person, or object).

Then tell the children what you do with it.

Last ask what do I spy?

Children will be given four guesses and then the teacher will show the picture and children will say what it was. Keep doing this until you have gone through the pictures.

Next time you play let one child at a time see the picture and ask the questions. Play continues with the children each doing one picture and then another child will take a turn.

You can use this game often and keep it fun by changing the picture sets that you use in the pocket.

## What's That Sound?

Make a recording of ten different sounds around your home, such as the water running, the T.V. playing and the mixer running. Children will listen to the sounds and try to guess what they heard. When the child guesses correct, give the child a small sticker and have them put it on their own index card. When they have listened to all the sounds have them count how many stickers they have. Then listen again to the same tape and have them put their stickers this time on the other side. Tell them to see if they can get more than they did last time. When finished listening the second time, have them count the number of stickers and see if they got more right this time.

**My Name Letter Sound**

Prepare a large balloon first letter for each child's name. Children will glue beans inside their balloon letter, while forming their first letter. Next children will take turns pointing to their letter, while all the children make the sound of that letter. Then each child will take a turn saying their letter sound by themselves.

**Shaving Cream Letters**

Put an apron and a tray in front of each child at the table. Children will practice writing their names in the shaving cream with their finger on their own tray. Have a laminated name strip for each one to copy their own name. Children will say the letters in their name one at a time to the teacher before leaving the table. While they are waiting for their turn, they will practice their letters or draw shapes.

# FREE TIME

## CREATIVE ARTS

Draw and cut out large monsters and put them on a table for children to finger paint on. The finger paint will be made from small boxes of instant pudding. Prepare as usual, but add about 1/4 to 1/3 cup more milk. Use colors like chocolate pudding or use vanilla pudding and color the pudding with food coloring. See monster example.

Use poster paint on the easel with large pieces of watercolor paper. Let children paint the letters in their names and make designs around their name.

## SENSORY

Put warm water in the sensory table with a small amount of dish soaps to make bubbles in the water. Also put different sizes of bottles, scoops and funnels so they can pour and discover amounts that of water that will fit inside the different sizes of bottles.

Put purple slime into a pail in your sensory table. Use 1 part water to 2 parts of corn starch and add enough purple poster paint to make it colored or choose a color that the children will like. Mix the poster paint with a little dish soap before mixing with the cornstarch. The Mixture will look solid, but it will run through your fingers if you hold it. Adjust as needed by adding a little more water of cornstarch. Be sure and remind children to wipe off the slime with their hands before leaving the table to wash their hands.

## DRAMATIC PLAY & SOCIAL DEVELOPMENT

Collect and put blankets and pillows in this area, so that children can pretend to go to bed. An old alarm clock would be great if they could set the alarm. You could also use robes, large P.J.s and large night gowns. It's important to make them large enough so they can wear them over their cloths. Also include lots of stuffed animals and baby dolls. Have clothing for the dolls to wear especially night clothing, diapers and baby bottles. Have rocking chairs so they can rock the babies to sleep.

## SCIENCE

Place books about stars, moons and planets on the table for them to look through. Add glow in the dark stars to the ceiling. Then put several small flashlights on the table. Let children turn off the light by that table so they can see the stars glow. They can also shine the flash lights around that part of the room in the dark.

Put an assortment of different types of magnets and items to be repelled and attracted by the magnets. Encourage children to explore what happens when you put two magnets together. Then turn one of the magnets around the other way and see what happens.

## GROSS MOTOR SKILLS

### Balance Beam Fun

Children will take turns walking forward and sideways on a balance beam holding their stuffed animal.

### Monster Hunt

Draw a large monster. Then attach it behind a box for children to use as a target. Next, hide the monster in the classroom or outside. Also make a masking tape line about three feet away from the monster. Then prepare a sack to carry bean bags for the children to use.

Tell the children to tiptoe very quietly behind her/him because there is a (pretend) monster in the room. The class will follow the teacher around the room or go outside behind the teacher while tiptoeing. They will keep following the teacher until they see the monster. Then the children will sneak up to the monster, still tiptoeing.

Now children will each be given a bean bag and told to stand behind the masking tape line. Next each child will take a turn throwing the bean bag at the monster. Tell children to go to the back of the line when they have had a turn. When all children have had a turn, tell them that they may take one more turn.

## FIELD TRIP IDEAS

Make arrangements for children to attend a planetarium. Invite parents to come with your class on this field trip. Go over the field trip safety rules before going and be sure and take your camera with you to take pictures of the children and the parents that go with you on this adventure.

# Where To Get What You Need

There are many different places to get what you need. If you use your imagination, many items can be substituted for what you have on hand, can get for free, etc. For example, you may have an abundance of baby food jars from a family toddler. You can easily convert these to be part of a project. Teaching is also about being resourceful. Have family, friends, students and yourself save:

- Baby food jars

- Toilet paper rolls

- Paper towel rolls

- Scraps of material

- Extra tile

- Extra pieces from home improvement projects

- Coffee cans

- Oatmeal containers

- 2 liter bottles

- Cereal boxes

- Egg carton

- Milk jugs

- Salt containers

- Anything you can think of to be re-purposed for a learning tool


Other places to get materials include:

- Home improvement stores (Lowes or Home Depot)

- Dollar Stores

- Educational Supply Stores

- Grocery Store

- Party Supply Store

- Online Resources:

  — Oriental Trading Company: www.orientaltrading.com

  — http://www.etacuisenaire.com

  — Many great songs and activities are available from http://www.newbridgeonline.com/, which is where you can find the MacMillan Sing and Learn songs and other activities. Use the search function and type in "songs for learning". You may also be able to find these used online at www.alibris.com, www.amazon.com, or www.abebooks.com.

www.ingramcontent.com/pod-product-compliance
Lightning Source LLC
LaVergne TN
LVHW081320060426
835509LV00015B/1598